"Silly Women"

"Silly Women"

Rita Jones Rushing

Silly Women

Italics quotation is the authors emphasis
Bold quotation is the authors emphasis
Underlined quotation is the authors emphasis

Scriptures quotations are taken from Life Application
Study Bible, NLT, Copyright © 1988,1989,1990, 1991,1993,
1996, 2009 by Tyndale House Publishers, Incorporated.
Used by permission.

Scripture quotations are taken from The New King James
Version of the Bible. Copyright © 1997, 1980, 1982, by
Thomas Nelson, Inc., Publishers. Used by permission.

Poem taken from Divinely Inspired, Copyright © 1998,
by Cynthia Jaurdon-Simmons.

Other poems written by Rita Jones Rushing, Kaylo
L. Henry and Cynthia J. Simmons copyright © 2009.
Used by permission

To order additional copies of this book, contact:
Xlibris Corporation
1-888-795-4274
www.Xlibris.com
Orders@Xlibris.com
64178

Contents

DEDICATIONS

This book is dedicated to the God of Abraham, Isaac and Jacob. May the words you've given me be a blessing to all who read.

To my mother, Zola Mae Causey who loved me and recognized the difference in me. I will carry her memory with me always, as I seek the things of God!

Acknowledgements

Dr. Samantha Ackers

Phillip Bessix for all of his technological wisdom.

To all my family and friends who believed in me, prayed for me, and supported me. This book is just one of the many things you have helped me to accomplish. Keep praying for me and keep trusting God.

Introduction

Most people don't want to be alone. In fact, if they were completely honest, they would say they are lonely and, some are terrified of being alone. The thought of being alone often result in some women starting or remaining in relationships that are not of God. When this happens it ties God's hands from, sending that woman the man that God has chosen and often times it can put a wedge between them and God.

God does not object to us having a mate, in fact, He created a mate for Adam, and her name was Eve. When God created Eve for Adam, this union became the first union of marriage. God created the institution of marriage, and He offers marriage as a blessing to us that belong to Him.

There are those who acknowledge they belong to God, but in actuality their behavior differs from their confession. They pretend to be Christians around other Christians and behave like they are unsaved around others.

These are the same women who attend church faithfully, sing in the choir and serve on various committees in the church.

Women and men, who are truly of God, can no longer be identified as to who are the daughters of God, and who are the daughters of Satan! We cannot observe what we see in a church setting and declare that she is holy and Godly just because she is waving *"holy hands"*. Godliness is not a Sunday occurrence.

Godliness is a <u>lifestyle</u>. It is a lifestyle that should be displayed in the public where all can see as well as in privacy where no one can see.

This book is designed to edify, encourage, inspire and insert positive element in women to change their lifestyle through The Word of God, prayer and self-examination. *I have changed my lifestyle and I know that you can too!* However, you must be forewarned, *Silly Women* is " *raw*", *"cut throat"* and just *"plain talk"*. Through this book, readers will be challenged to consider how God's Word relates to their personal relationships, lifestyle, and to persuade <u>us</u> to be obedient to God's commandments.

May this book be a blessing to you as you wait on the promises of God.

Chapter 1

COMPETITION

From the time a female child is a little girl she, has vied for and received the attention of a male. Little girls who were blessed to grow up in a home with both parents would always run to their fathers whenever they wanted something. She knew her father would always say "yes", "even when mother said" no," and no was not an option from him. When she had a cold, all daddy had to do was step into her room and she would recover immediately, long before her mother would start cooking her special homemade soup. Fathers would always make their daughters feel special by telling them that were "daddy's heart or daddy's baby". From that time on women have tried to capture and retain a man's heart, only to feel special or be shown love.

As the female child grew into a young adult, her attention shifted from wanting attention from her father to wanting attention from other males outside the home. She is aware that her body is changing and she realizes that she is now beginning to look like older women in the home as well as women outside her home. She is no longer interested in childish things, according to her, but she shows interest in things that would show her maturity. Even though her parents wished that she would remain childlike a little longer, she is eager for her parents to buy her clothing that is more stylish and up-to-date. Her argument is that everyone is wearing these fashions, and soon or later her parent or parents would give in to this nonsense. This argument which she wins creates and sets the stage for this young woman to become competitive with other young women.

Women are very competitive when it comes down to getting the attention of a male. So much so, they are willing to literally engage in physical combat or embarrass themselves and their families in order to <u>reel</u> in a man. Reality shows such as "Who Wants to Marry a Millionaire" or "The Bachelor" are two examples of women who competent for the main prize, which is a man. These women leave their jobs, families and friends to go on national television to make fools of themselves in order to get a man. They wear skimpy or revealing clothing to try and outdo one another in order to get the main prize, which is the man. Not only that, they are willing to <u>swap spit</u> with someone they know nothing about except the fact that he is single and available. And for some women, that's all they need to know. These women are not concerned whether or not they may get mononucleosis; which is an infectious virus transmitted through saliva or by sharing a glass or food utensil with someone who has mononucleosis. The only concern they have is he's available.

Women don't have to compete with other women to be noticed if this is God's divine mate for you. You *don't* and *won't* have to go on national television for God to lead that man to you, and you don't have to setup an appointment to meet him. God has a setup procedure that will surpass any meeting that any television producer can arrange. It's called a, *"Holy Ghost Setup."* You don't have to worry about competing with any other woman when God sets you up to meet your mate. The only thing you have to do is be patient and hold steadfast to the promises of God and prepare yourself like Esther did in the Bible. The Word of God says in **Esther 2: 12** *" she was given the prescribed twelve months of beauty treatments—six months with oil of myrrh, followed by six months with special perfumes and ointments."* In today's standards, we can say that Esther had a *"spa treatment."* I am more than sure her skin was soft as *"cotton"* and her feet were not *"crusty"* after such lengthy preparation. Esther prepared her body and her spirit while she waited to go before the king. Your preparation time is here. The only thing that you should be preparing for is the husband that God is going to send to you.

We must study the Word of God and keep our bodies and spirit ready for his arrival. So turn off the television, pray, read your Bible, and go and bath prepare yourself the way Esther did before she met her king!

COMPETITION

MY FRIEND IS HAVING A PARTY,
I WAS INVITED TO BE HER GUEST.

I'LL GO LOOK IN MY CLOSET,
TO FIND MY SUNDAY BEST.

I NEED TO CALL HER ON THE PHONE AND ASK WILL THERE BE
MEN?
IF SHE TELLS ME YES IN HER ANSWER, I KNOW I'M GONNA
SHOW SOME SKIN.

TODAY I FORGET ABOUT MODEST CLOTHING,
AND SHOW A LITTLE SKIN.
BECAUSE AFTER ALL THE PRIZE IS GREAT
IT'S A MAN IN THE END.

by
Rita Jones Rushing

Chapter 2

LONELINESS

There is a big difference in being lonely and being alone. Loneliness is when you have a void in your heart that says something is missing. You can be in a room full with people, yet you feel lonely. Being alone is when someone is " alone" and there is no other living being in the room or area surrounding you.

Whenever people have a *"void"* in their lives, they try to fill it with people, or things. Often times, women of God will entertain conversations or become involved in relationships to fill that void, even if it means pursuing a relationship with non-Christians men. If you asked them why they are spending so much time with these men who are not saved, they are quick to say, *"Girl I'm trying to minister to him and bring him to the Lord"*, or *" girl it's just somebody to talk to."* If you need someone to talk too, talk to God. The Word of God says in **John 14:18, *"I (God) will not you leave you comfortless: I will come to you."*** Woman of God you need to stop lying to yourself and others and just tell the truth! The only thing you're trying to do is bring that man into your arms and maybe down the *"aisle"* in matrimony. But let me warn you, it is easier for that unsaved man to pull you back into the *"world"* than it is for you to bring him into the kingdom of God. There are demonic forces working on him trying to keep him in the world, and demonic forces working trying to pull you back into the world! You probably say that you won't ever return or go back into the world, but temptation is everywhere and even Satan tried to tempt Jesus, so who are you!

I know I have gone through enough *stuff* and fought a lot of battles in my lifetime, and I *do not* want to battle again. I know that God has equipped us to battle the enemy, but girlfriend, this is not be your battle. If you are an evangelist and God has *called you* to minister to that man and cast out those demons, then I say do what God has equipped you to do. Because whoever God calls, he equips with the *"Holy Spirit."* But if God didn't call you to minister to that man, you are on your own, and heaven help you. Don't look for God to back you up while you are playing those games.

Some women of God believe it is their mission in life to find a man and get married. So much so, some are willing to forfeit or give up everything they know that lines up with the Word of God. The Word of God is full of inspirations for women who are without a mate and who believe God for the promise. So many women either *don't believe* the Word of God, or they are *not willing* to wait. Some women try and manipulate the wait time and take matters in their own hands. It's like they are saying, *"God you are taking too long."* Another reason women try to manipulate or speed up the timing of God to send them a mate, is because they *don't fully trust God to deliver.* So what do they do? These **"silly women"** take matters into their own hands.

One of the ways they take matters into their own hands is to bribe or buy a man into a relationship. What I mean by this statement is, women will prepare expensive meals or buy little gifts in hopes this man will become interested in them. The meals and the gifts are indications there are more meals and gifts to come in a relationship with you. You may say, *"well it wasn't much, just a 99 cents greeting card".* But why are you buying him a greeting card after spending an hour or two in his company? It is not necessary for you to pursue him. Let him pursue you and allow *him* to send you the greeting card and gifts at an appropriate time.

When one person is attracted to the opposite sex, that person will think about him or her for hours on hours in a day. If the attraction is one-sided, on the side of the woman, she will go into a combative mode to try and secure her target. She often tries to use telepathy or, read his mind to try and figure out whether or not he is thinking about her. Hinting around is normal for her and she ask such questions as, *"what did you do today?"* She could care less what he did today. What you really want to know is whether or not he thought about you today.

Some women are so good at asking questions, they could work for the FBI or the CIA, two agencies that ask a lot of questions and investigates the person. Oh, I'm sorry, I take that back, so women avoid certain questions. Questions they *should ask, they don't ask,* and questions they *shouldn't ask* they ask!

Women are very good at hinting around or playing mind games to find out a man's plans. Every woman likes to be remembered on her birthday and on Valentine's Day, even if you're not willing to admit it. So women will pretend it does matter to them whether or not they receive something on that special day. If she truly honest with herself, the celebration of those special days are important to her. Those special days started when she was a child. The thought of someone thinking about her, or doing something for her has not disappeared. So instead of admitting that she wishes to be thought of on that special day, she will just use another tactic. She will start to throw little hints to suggest some special day is coming. When she doesn't receive a gift she will play it off as if it *didn't* matter, yet her heart is breaking inside.

Women have always been the main caretakers of the family. In fact, she is well aware of the importance of the mother and aware of the role that other family members play in a relationship. In the 1960's, when young ladies came of age to start dating, either the father or mother or both parents would question the young man. The parent would ask the young man, *"who are your folks?"* The parents would either *approve* or *disapprove* of the relationship. If the young man had serious intentions about the young lady, he would then take her home to meet *his* parents for approval. In those days both families had to *approve* of the relationship.

Today, meeting the family is still important except the roles have reversed and it is the woman who wants to meet the family. She will ask and keep asking, *"when are you going to take me to meet your family?"* She is ready to meet and greet and willing to put her best foot forward. She will show every good tooth in her mouth, be complimentary to his parent or parents and any other family member. She will be very attentive in his family surrounding, making sure that she notes his likes and dislikes, as well as all of his family members. She will make sure that she finds out what his mother likes and dislikes. She is aware of the fact that if his mother likes her, then she has become the newest member of his family! She will go out of her way to purchase gifts for his family in order for them to tell him, *"oh she is so nice or she is so sweet."* Sometimes being *"nice"* and *"sweet"* comes with a cost!

Sometimes these gifts are not always paid for with money. Some women will volunteer to babysit for his nieces and nephews or complete other duties as assigned. These women will run errands, cook meals and clean the *whole* house for him and his relatives. That includes toilets and all. Honestly, I don't like cleaning toilets, not even my own. But this is a task that must be done for sanitary purposes. If it pleases you to clean other people houses and toilets, have at it! It's okay to help someone if that person needs *your* help. But if that person has not asked for your help, stop volunteering. Stop and look around your own home and start cleaning your own house. Go in your own closet and clean that space, sweep under your own bed and stop throwing yourself on his family. Those folk are *not interested* in you at all. The only interest they have in you, is what they can get from you, or the *service* you can provide! So stop being sub servant to another human being and try to become servant to God! It is much easier being a *servant* to God than it is to another *human* being. God will give you at least one day of rest!

LONELINESS

When I open my eyes in the morning,
I can hear the birds sing,

I look to my right,
there's no one sleeping next to me.

Years of being alone has made me sad,
When I see couples together,
sometimes I get mad!

I say to God, "What about me?"
He says, "Just be patient my dear, I have something for thee."

His words are assuring in times like these,
when loneliness reappears,
I fall on my knees.

by
Rita J. Rushing

Chapter 3

FLIP THE SCRIPT

Women all over the world have female friends they share in-depth details of their personal lives. But do women go too far in what they say to their friends? Women tell other women all of their personal business, including telling men their personal business as well. When a woman meets a man, she is ready to start her motor, and start running off at the mouth, in hopes of capturing and maintaining that man's attention. When a man meets a woman, if he is interested in her, the first thing he asks is her name. When he ask her name, it is usually the first sign he is interest in getting to know her. In the past, the man is usually the person who takes control of the conversation and *not* the woman. Women today get so excited that a man has *stopped her* to engage in a conversation, *she will start* the conversation. She does this because she is so excited that this man has stopped her to start a conversation. As the conversation goes on, he will pop the big question of inquiry, *"are you married"*? She responds to the question, either yes or no. Then the next question from him is *"can I have your telephone number"*? Some are willing to give men more than just their telephone number on their first encounter. They give their names, addresses, home and work telephone numbers without knowing anything about this stranger. They don't know whether he is a serial killer, rapist, or robber. And let's not forget that he may be a child molester trying to get to know you, only to be after your child or children. Men are not giving you their *home* telephone number *only* their cell telephone number. Perhaps it is because he is a married man, or shacking with a woman. Don't fall for the cell phone game!

But why do women allow men to ask all the questions and control the flow of the conversation? I believe that women are too afraid to ask men questions for fear of possibly losing a man who is interested in her. So instead, women allow him to ask all the questions.

As women of God, women *cannot* longer allow men to ask all the questions without asking questions of their own. Women need to ask men questions to find out whether they are talking to *"Sons of God"* or *"Sons of Satan!"* You should start asking questions and *"flip the script."*

Women are now able to *"flip the script"* and ask questions without being viewed as controlling or *"out of place."* The next time a man comes up to a woman of God and asks her name, she should be prepared to *"flip the script."* Now that he has made the first move and asked your name, turn around and ask him if *he is married.* I didn't say ask him *his name,* I said asks him *"if he is married!"* If he says that he is married, tell him to have a bless day and move on. But if he says that he is single, continue *your* questioning and continue to *"flip the script."* Now comes the clincher, ask him if knows *Jesus.* Not only that, but asks him if he knows *Jesus* and if he has a *personal relationship* with Jesus Christ. Don't stop there, but continue to probe and asks him whether or not he attends church regularly. Start talking about the Bible and ask him if he tithes. If he stumbles or hesitates with any of these answers, bid him farewell and wish him Godspeed! Don't hesitate in dismissing yourself from his presence. If you are a Christian woman, you have nothing in common with this man. The Bible tells us in **II Corinthians 6:14 says, *"Be ye not unequally yoked together with unbelievers: for what fellowship hath righteousness with unrighteousness? And what communion hath light with darkness?"*** Don't think that you can change him while you getting to know him. It will be time consuming while you try and convert him into the things of God. There are women of God who have married men who were not saved or Christians, and now they are trying to convert these men to becoming Christians. Trying to bring someone you love to Christ can be very difficult and it can also put a strain on the marriage or on the relationship. I have known of women who have tried to bring unsaved men to God. Please believe me when I say it can be quite a chore, especially when he is not ready to seek God for himself. It requires a lot of work and a lot of prayer. But you don't have to work at all to convert the man God has for you. God has the perfect man for you that already knows and loves Him and his son Jesus Christ; a man who tithes, attends church and reads his Bible. This man has already sought God for himself and the only thing you have to do is wait upon the *Lord* to *arrange* the meeting place for the two of you. Jesus said in **Matthew 7:33,** *"But seek ye first the kingdom of God, and his righteousness; and all these thing shall be added unto you."* When the Word of God says that all things shall be added unto you; that includes a man of God that will be richly added to your life at God's appointed time!

FLIP THE SCRIPT

WORDS HAVE ALWAYS BEEN EASY FOR ME,
EVEN UNTIL THIS DAY.
BUT OFTEN TIMES I AM SPEECHLESS,
AND I DONT KNOW WHAT TO SAY.

AS LONG AS I AM AROUND WOMEN,
MY WORDS JUST EASLY FLOW.
BUT WHEN A HANDSOME MAN COMES AROUND,
I AM HEADED FOR THE DOOR.

HE'LL BEGIN WITH ASKING QUESTIONS,
AND MAKE ME FORGET MY NAME.
I SAY MY NAME IS WANDA,
I HOPE HE'S NOT PLAYING A GAME.

MAYBE I SHOULD ASK HIM QUESTIONS,
TO SEE WHAT HE WILL SAY.
BECAUSE I KNOW IF HE STUMBLES
I WILL BE ON MY WAY.

by
Rita J. Rushing

Chapter 4

SEX AND THE SINGLE GIRL

If you are in a relationship with a person, are you intimate with that person? When we think about intimacy, what is the first thing that comes to your mind? For some, it may be kissing, for others it may be foreplay. For the majority of women it is, *sex!* For single women of God, sex can be a *killer* if you are having sex with someone you are not married to by law and in the sight of God.

If you are a single woman of God and you are having sex outside of marriage, it has an adverse affect on you. But the most adverse affect it will have on you will be how it affects your relationship with *God!* God is not pleased when women have sex outside of marriage, and when that happens, you *kill the relationship* you have with God. The Word of God tells us in **I Corinthians 6:18-20,** *"Run away from sexual sin. No other sin so clearly affects the body as this one does. For sexual immorality is a sin against your own body. Or don't you know that your body is the temple of the Holy Spirit, who lives in you and was given to you by God! You do not belong to yourself, for God bought you with a high price. So you must honor God with your body."* It's not that God don't want women of God to have sex, but He wants us to have sex with our *husband and not every Tom, Dick and Harry!* Women should be very, very careful when having sex with others, because you don't know who that person is sleeping with while he is sleeping with you. Some folk having sex believe it is some type of game and it's okay to be care free and have casual sex. But casual sex can cost you to lose your life. It is unfortunate that so many people have to find out the hard way about having sex without the benefits of marriage.

There are a lot of single women who are looking for a husband. They believe if they sleep with that man he will want to marry her. But I beg to differ from that belief! A man does not want a women that he can have sex with at any given time or place. He is only waiting to see how long it will take before he is intimate with you; and if you are willing to wait until marriage. Some men suggest having sex before marriage in order to see whether or not the sex is good. Women also bring up the subject of having sex before marriage. Someone once asked me will I have sex before marriage. She girl, "don't you want to *"test it"* before you marry him?" I said, *"No."* "Suppose he can't do nothing!" I said, "girl if he can't do nothing, then I know **My God** can fix something that is broken!" Then she goes and says, "suppose he want to *"test you"* before he marries you?" I said, " I am not a car that I should be test driven by a man, and I will not sleep with a man before I say, "I do." This is my position on sex before marriage. As for me, no sex period! I was not created by General Motors to be *"test"* driven, I was created by God to be loved. When someone is looking to buy a car, we all know that person *does not* purchase the first car they *test* drive. They keep searching until they find the car they can *"afford"* and the best deal in town. Each and every time they go to a different dealership, they *test* drive the car. At the end of that day, that person may have *test* driven over ten cars. Imagine those cars being you. Often times the person walks away from the dealership empty *" handed."* It is the same with women. The man walks away from your body, *"emptied"* handed, without making a commitment to you. The dealership does not lose a *"thing"* when someone test drives their vehicles. The cars on the lot are usually *"demonstrators"* to be used to *test* drive. At the end of year all *"demonstrators"* are sold at a *"depreciated cost."* Those *"demonstrators"* are sold *"as is"* and with *"high mileage."* Honey, don't let anyone put those *"extra miles"* on you and *"depreciate"* your value! Just close your legs!

There is an old saying, "why buy the cow when you can get the milk for free." Some women have allowed so many farmers **(men)** to milk the cow, get the milk, sell the milk and make a profit in the end. Think about this! If a man is sleeping with you without the benefits of marriage he is milking you for all that you are worth. **He is getting the same sexual benefits from you without being married to you.** Why buy the cow!. **He gets the milk each and every time you open your legs without the benefit of marriage to him.** Why buy the cow! **He sells you out when he goes and talk about what it was like milking his cow to his friends.** Now his friends want to milk his cow for the same benefits he received. Everyone will know what you were wearing while he was milking the cow. He is now selling the milk of his cow! **He is selling you out by disclosing your personal business with all who will listen**. He makes a profit from the cow (woman) when you keeping allowing him to sleep. He profits by not making a commitment to you. He can keep buying cows all over the city and keep his profits (income) with no commitment to you and no one else. He can keep his money in his pocket and still profit. The profit he is getting is free sex with no commitment. He has all the benefits of having his own cow without having to feed the cow, shelter the cow from any storms, or having to package the milk carton (buying clothing or etc) for the cow. Are you a cow? God did not created you and me to be barnyards animals. And not only that, the most valuable animal to any farmer is the cow!

God is delighted when women of God have sex with *their spouses.* Sex is not just for reproduction, but it is also for bonding love and overall enjoyment between husbands and wives. Don't allow having sex outside of marriage to kill your relationship with God. Instead, walk away from fornication and walk with God. Also, stop using those sex toys for self-gratification as well. I understand that sometimes our hormones rage as though they were on *"fire"*, but we must pray to contain the fire. The Word of God says in **I Corinthians 9,** *"But if they cannot contain, let them marry; for it is better to marry than to burn."* God already knows what you have desire of, and that includes sex. So I say pray and ask God to let your sexual desires lie dormant. Wait until God sends your husband to stir up your desires as a woman. And then you can ask God to help you bring pleasure to your husband, *not her husband,* but your husband! If God has not sent your husband to you, then your body is not your own! It belongs to the Lord! The Word of God says in **I Corinthians 6:13,** " . . ."*Now the body is not for fornication, but for the Lord; and the Lord for the body."* The next time someone want to have sex with you, tell them you must first ask permission from the Lord. Tell them if the Lord *ain't* saying *"nothing"* . . . . then I *ain't* *"doing"* nothing! Amen!

SEX AND THE SINGLE GIRL

NUMBER 1, 2 OR 3,
I WONDER OF THEM WHICH ONE IS ME.
I THOUGHT I HAD HIM TO MYSELF, BUT TO MY SURPRISE,
HE HAD TWO OTHER SETS OF CHOCOLATE THIGHS.

HE'LL COME TO ME AND BITE A PIECE, BUT NOT SATISFY HIS
MEAL,
FOR WHEN HE LEFT MY HOUSE, HE WAS HUNGRY STILL.

I WENT TO THE DOCTOR TO CHECK ON THIS ITCH,
AND I SAW HIM IN THE ARMS OF THE ONE HE SAID HE
DITCHED.

OUT OF THE OFFICE CAME ANOTHER TO OUR SURPRISE,
THE THIRD WOMAN OF HIS, WITH TEARS IN HER EYES.

SHE WENT TO HIM AND SAID, "WHAT HAVE YOU DONE TO ME?"
"THE DOCTOR SAID THE TEST WAS POSITIVE, I HAVE H.I.V"

by
Kaylo L. Henry

Chapter 5

ADULTERY, IS IT FOR YOU?

Being lonely can cause some women, even women of God to forget whose they are, and who they are. Women are willing to stoop to levels far below the standards of God and below their *own* standards. These standards are reduced in order to fill the voids of *loneliness*, *lack of sex* and *having someone to love them*. Because of these voids women of God form relationships with men who are non-Christians, on drugs or alcohol, bi-sexual, gamblers, and etc.

Some of these desperate women will go so far as to *"rob the cradle"* and become involve with men young enough to be their own children. They form relationships with their children's classmates or younger. When that happens these women rob these young men of bedroom experiences. Those type of experiences should only come from him getting to know *his* own wife and vice versa. Don't bring your bedroom experience to these young men to prove a point that you can have a sexual or long term relationship with a younger man. Allow these young men to learn what to do, and allow him and his wife to learn together.

Women who become involved with married men are fighting two losing battles; one with trying to break up the marriage, and the other with God. God created the institution of marriage and how dare anyone try to come between the union of that man and his wife. I have heard some women say *"some man is better than no man, even if he belongs to someone else."* Yes, these women say that now, but what will they say before God on the Day of Judgment?

I know some women have ventured into this forbidden relationship. *I too* was once in a forbidden relationship. **Silly, Silly Me!** It was with a younger man who was fine in every since of the word. For many years we noticed each other in social setting but we never engaged in a conversation, always just a smile. One day he approached me and we became friends instantly. One day *we* decided to become intimate, which was the worst thing we could have done. Again, **Silly, Silly, Me!** The intimacy was short lived. Each time I had sex with him, I would have horrible nightmares. Little did I know at the time that God had a call on my life. Not only that, I was losing sleep. I was intimate with this man three to five times and each time I would have horrible dreams. I remember one night I dreamed that women were *"throwing stones"* at me and calling me a *"whore and home wrecker."* That did it for me! **I felt this was how God saw me in His sight as a *"whore and home wrecker."*** I called him over after that horrible dream and told him that I **Did Not** want to see him anymore. He questioned me about my decision to breakup with him. He thought it was because he could not spend enough time with me, or because I wanted to see someone else. I told him my decision had nothing to do with me wanting to see someone else. I told him that each time I slept with him, the *Holy Spirit "whipped me."* I informed him that it was not just a few bad dreams, but it was almost every night whether we were intimate or not. *I just wanted to make peace with God, have peace with myself and get a good night sleep.* He tried to convince me that everyone have bad dreams, but my answer to him was, *"you are not the one being convicted of sexual sin and losing sleep."* I told him that God wanted me to come out of that sinful mess that he and I both shared. He said he understood and respected my decision to end the sexual relationship, but days later he called and I didn't answer the telephone. For weeks and months he would call my house during the middle of the night or knock on my door at wee hours in the morning. When he would knock on my door, I would not open my door but I would peep out the window and see that it was him. One night he came to my home around two o'clock in the morning. I finally opened the door after months of his knocking. I was tired of this man knocking on my door, calling my home and breaking my rest! God had already *returned* to me a peaceful sleep once I ended the relationship. Now he was breaking my rest by calling and knocking on my door. I was so angry with him, but more with myself, because of the mess I created! **Silly Me!** Although he said he understood that I wanted to get my life straight with God, he really could care less. I could tell that he cared less, so I had to *"jump"* into street mode. Forget the spiritual things of God for a moment, I had to get him straight in a way that only a worldly man could understand. I let him into my home and he thought he had finally broke me down, and now he was back in my arms and in my bed. I told him that if he called my house one more time, and knocked on my door one more time, that I would call his wife. I would tell her my name, give her my address and tell her where his birthmark was on his upper thigh! He was shocked that I would make such a threat, but the look in my eyes told him that I meant business! Sometimes when we try to convey to worldly people that we are no longer in the flesh, and were are trying to do what is pleasing to God, they don't understand. He did not seem to get it when I said that I was becoming a born again Christian. He did not see the change in me because he had not been around me. I bet he *got his mind right and his hormones together* when I told him that I would call his wife. Sometimes you got to get a person's mind right, and I was not the one to play with! Play with me if you want too, see what will happen! Don't ever try to persuade me to go back to the way of the world, because I will fight you to the bitter end! God forgave me for my mess, and now you won't take "No" for an answer, I don't think so! Although I had no intentions of calling his wife, I had to threatened him in order for him to leave me alone. He left me alone for good and I had no more problems with him. I prayed and asked God to forgive me and I know that I am forgiven. The Word of God says in **Isaiah 43:25**, *"I, yes, I alone will blot out your sins for my sake and never think of them again."* If God <u>will not</u> remember my sexual sin from that adulterous affair, then I <u>will not</u> remember it as well. The only reason it was called back from my memory, was for the purpose of other **"Silly Women."** God said, *"Tell about your adulterous affair."* I did what I was told to do, because I want to be obedient to God! All is forgiven!

For those of you who <u>have not</u> had a relationship with a married man, I say don't be silly like **ME.** For those of you who are having an affair with a married man, I say repent and sin no more. It is not as though you cannot get out of this relationship. All you have say is, *"go home to your wife and children and don't ever come back."* Don't just say don't come back, because he will come back. You must also be willing to back those words up with action. Once you stop him from coming to your house, that relationship will be over. For you and I both know that you will not be going to his house. The only way you go to his house is if you are on a *"suicide mission"* and you are ready to meet *"Your maker"!*

Adulterous affairs has destroyed and literally killed family members who were innocent and not at fault. Being in an adulterous affair can cause divorce, psychological problems, and rob children of growing up in a two-parent home because of the sexual sins of one or both parents. It can also cause injury to members of the *immediate* family, as well as *long term friends.* It is not rare to hear of adulterous affairs between close knit friends. Close knit friends often form friendships and go places together in groups. The couples arrange their schedules to include other couples as well. In the end one of the spouses ends up in bed with the other close friend's husband or wife. The couples became too familiar with one another and someone, or both parties, saw an opportunity to *"dip"* with another person's spouse. Once intimacy starts, it will destroy the *"whole couple thing,"* even those *who may not* be guilty or have any intentions on becoming intimate with anyone in the couples group. Another such act of adultery that can occur, is within the *immediate* family. It is unfortunate with all of the men on planet earth that some women has to sleep with their sister's husband, daughter's husband or stepfather. This list is not limited to those stated but also any man that is close to one of the family members. The innocent woman may think everyone is getting along as a close family, but in the end she will later find out her sister is sleeping with her husband. Maybe this is the reason why the two of them will volunteer to go the store together for forgotten grocery items. Or perhaps it is the reason why the mother-in-law cooks such wonderful meals for her son-in-law. When the discovery is made of these adulterous affairs, it *"pits"* family members against family members and everybody loses in the end.

Adultery is a serious charge, so much so that God wrote this commandment in **Deuteronomy 5:17-18** *"Thou shalt not kill, neither shalt thou commit adultery"*. What part of *thou shalt not* do you not understand? You can't say that you didn't know that adultery was a sin. You knew it but you continued to ignore The Word of God. You did what you wanted to do just like I did! **Silly Me!** Don't think that you're getting off free even if no one knows about the adulterous affair. Adultery is *not* free. It will cost you in the end. You will pay for your affair!

The Word of God also says in Hebrews 10:26, *" For if we sin willfully after that we have received the knowledge of the truth, there remaineth no more sacrifice for sins."* What that means is, if you continue to sin after you receive the knowledge of the sin, then there is no longer a sacrifice for sins. *In other words, don't expect God to forgive you when you know what you are doing is wrong!* The only thing you can expect from God is a terrifying judgment by God.

When we slight any of God's commandments, we are trampling upon the blood of Jesus Christ. We put Him to shame, and mock His blood when we are disobedient to His commandments.

We are each responsible for our own behavior and will bear the consequences now and on the Day of Judgment. Ask yourself the question, "can you justify before God why you slept with that man when the Word of God says "run away from sexual sin.?" Don't give me your answer, tell it to God!

ADULTERY

WAS THAT YOUR HUSBAND YOU INTRODUCED TO ME,
CAZ' I COULD HAVE SWORN HE WAS MARRIED TO SALLY B.

I MET THEIR CHILDREN, I THINK THEY HAVE FOUR,
SO WHY OUT OF WEDLOCK YOU TRYING TO GIVE HIM MORE?

THE BIBLE SAYS THE BEDROOM IS UNDEFILED,
WHORES AND ADULTERS WILL BE JUDGED AT THE TRIAL.

SO ASK GOD'S FORGIVENESS, AND SIN NO MORE,
AND STOP THAT MAN FROM COMING IN YOUR DOOR.

by
Kaylo L. Henry

Chapter 6

What Are You Wearing Woman of God

Everything we see today centers on sex. The media plays a major role in flaunting sex in our face on a daily basis. But why not, we all know that sex sells. We are bombarded by magazine advertisements and television commercials that show more of the flesh and less of the product. It is not necessary for a company to show me half-naked women in their advertisement in order for me to purchase their product. If the product is good, the product will sell itself. Companies that advertise products showing women with low cleavage, short skirts, or tight fitting clothing go too far to in advertising their product. Thirty years ago, the media wouldn't dare advertise products that suggested anything but the product itself. The company would be afraid of an *"outcry"* from the viewing public and the product being removed from the shelves.

Women today are brazen in their apparel and more competitive than ever before. Not only are some of them brazen, but bold as well. Some are so bold that they wear short, tight—fitting, clothing to their child's school, to their job, as well as to the house of God. Some women of God go and sit in God's house wearing clothing so provocative, it would tempt the father of temptation, Satan himself! They intentionally wear short dresses with no *"draws"* and no *"pantyhose."* They sit, purposely, on the first pew of the church with their legs *"gapped"* wide opened, *"stanking up"* God's house. I didn't say *"stinking"*! They take a sit on the front row to try and tempt the men of God who are singing in the choir or in the pulpit. Baby, close your legs in God's house! Sometimes their dresses or blouses are so low-cut you would think they are going to breast-feed their babies in the sanctuary, and there is no babies in their arms.

I don't know whether she knows it, but trying to tempt a man on "*holy ground*" is dangerous business! These women with these filthy objectives or motives should take their temptations elsewhere and *not try* and defile God's house! The church should have the "*old sisters*" to guard the sanctuary for women who come in God's house half naked. You know the church ladies who wear all white outfits and sit in the front of the church. Give those half naked women those **"big scarves"** to cover their bosoms and legs. That will stop them! This would break up a lot of them from coming to God's house like they are going to a strip party. Also have all the ushers to direct **"those defilers"** to sit on the back row with all the ushers. This way the pastor won't have to **see** between "*their legs*" while preaching his powerful sermon. Let those men in the choir sing to God without having to look at "*that mess.*" These women are trying to keep those man from singing "*Holy praises to God.*" Shame on you! Don't say "*he shouldn't be looking.*" Don't act crazy, he's a man! He is going to look!

If these women are not careful they could be stricken with a stroke or heart attack at any given moment, while trying to tempt men in God's house. If you know of someone who is trying to tempt men in God's house, I suggest that you sit someplace else in the church to keep you from being in the *line of fire.* Do you remember what happen to the tribes of Korah, Dathan, and Abram in **Numbers 16: 23-36?** All three tribes where swallowed up alive because they had angered God! Don't think that God has lost His power to command the earth to open and swallow up people as He did in the *Old Testament.* The earth still has to obey God and if people are not careful, they will become *missing, and disappear without a trace!*

I know that you want to find a man of God, hopefully in God's house, but please cover yourself out of respect for God and for yourself. Keep in mind, you are not at your house, where you can be as brazen as you please, but you are in *God's house,* which is *Holy.* You may say you don't wear that type of clothing to church, but I am sure that some of you have some "*Hochee mama*" clothing in your closet. These are the clothes that you pull out of your closet when someone wants to take you on a date, or when you know you're going to a place where there will be lots of men, or *a man!* Right? These grown women have worn this type of clothing for so long, now their female daughters are coming to church with tight fitting clothes and low cleavage. Remember your children do what they see the parent or parents do!

Don't get me started! But as women of God, we don't have to try and market our "*wares*" or "*assets*" as a street vendor or like women of the world who are without shame. The Bible says in **I John 2:15-16,** " ***Love not the*** *world, neither the things that are in the world. If any man love the world, the love of the Father in not in him."* As women of God we should have a higher standard than women who are *not* of God. We must remember that when people see us, they should see the Christ in us and our clothing! Don't wear clothing that would cause others to stare or clothing that would be degrading to other Christian women. Whenever degrading occurs, respectability diminishes and it becomes a hard task to regain that respect. Ask yourself, "*to what degree of respectability* <u>should I</u> , *or* <u>can I</u> *demand from others because of my clothing?"* You must keep in mind that <u>*you*</u> are the person who shows others how to treat you in the first place, and your clothing says a lot about you. We must *walk, talk* and dress as a member of the royal family, and as children of the Most High God!

Don't misunderstand what I am saying about choice of clothing for women of God. I know there are some women who maybe homeless and have nothing to wear but the clothes on their backs. I am not talking about those women. Those women have no choice but to wear what they have. But for women who have choices, let their choices be one that is modest, descent and reflective of the God they serve.

Society says that we should *"dress to impress,"* but I say it is <u>not necessary</u> to try to impress the man that God has chosen for you! When God sends your help mate, you can be wearing a *"gunnysack"* and he will still think you are the most beautiful woman in the world. Do you remember the story in the **Book of Ruth** where Boaz noticed Ruth working in the fields from a distance? The Word of God says Boaz asks his foreman a question concerning Ruth, in **Ruth 2: 5,** ***Then Boaz asked his foreman, "who is that girl over there?"*** **And the foreman replied, "*She is the young woman from Moab who came back with Naomi.*"** Before Ruth went in the field do you think she went out to buy a new outfit to impress the men she would encounter? I don't think so! She wore what she had in her household and went about her business doing her work. Boaz noticed her from afar, and still married her, worn clothes and all! Women can learn a lot from that short story in the Word of God. Read it for yourself!

I know men are attracted to what they see but the question becomes, *"what is it we want them to see, and how much of it?"* As women of God we must remember that we should always be appropriately dress at all times. We should not dress like we are trying to attract the attention of every man walking on God's green earth. To be honest, I am not interested in every man who is interested in me. I am choosey! Okay, I said it, now you know. Yes I am choosey, but I only <u>chose</u> what God <u>chooses </u>for me. I am not interested in men who whistle at me to try and get my attention, like a master calling his dog. I don't entertain that type of behavior, nor do I wear clothing that would entice that kind of attention. Don't give the wolves (*men*) something to whistle about. Remember you are a sheep of *The Great Shepherd, Jesus Christ,* and Jesus don't whistle for us when he wants our attention, He calls us by our name. Keep in mind people who are not saved are *watching and waiting* for you to fall back to your old habits.

Those old habits or starting new habits will identify you with worldly things. Don't be concerned with worldly people who are watching what you wear. Be concerned and know that God is watching what you are wearing!

Chapter 7

YOU BETTER WATCH YOUR MOUTH !

Women and men not only look different, but the way they communicate is very different as well. Women, for the most part, talk more than men. In other words, women talk *too much!* Women can talk on the telephone for hours without taking a break to use the toilet or get a glass of water. This is due, in part, to the innovation of the cordless telephone. Women are longer stationary on the telephone, but they have the ability to cook a meal, eat, drink and use the toilet without ever having to hang up the telephone.

Women talk about everything under the sun and then some! Women talk about things of God and things that are *not* of God. Sometimes we talk so much we forget what we were talking about, or *whom we are talking too.* This is how they tell the secret they weren't suppose to tell! Some women of God talk about God, then they turn around and cuss like a sailor, all in the same breathe. If you talk to them long enough, they will tell you what kind of sex they had with their man during the week or over the weekend. You know what I'm talking about and don't act like you don't know what I am talking about. But how can they expect for God to bless them with their *filthy* mouth? Blessings and curses should *not* come out of the same mouth. I am more than sure that some people reading this book knows of family and friends who *"cuss like sailors." I know I do!* I have been in *"ear range"* of women whose speech is *"Godly"* around certain Christian women and that of a *"sailors daughter"* around others.

I know we all get angry at times and sometimes the *"old flesh"* will come up and out of us when we become angry. Back in September of 2008,

Hurricane Gustav drop a tree inside my house and I was forced to move. I hired a company out of New Orleans to move my furniture. Although the company had not completed the move, the drivers wanted the total cost before they would unload one piece of my furniture. Not only that, they wanted to be paid the full amount of over $1800.00 for that move. During this time all kinds of people and companies were *"ripping"* people off and taking their money, never to be seen again. I went to get a cashier's check for the movers while they supposedly unloaded my furniture at the storage unit. I stayed in line at Wal-Mart for about 45 minutes only to return and not one *"stick"* of my furniture was unloaded, and it was near dusk dark. The company wanted to be paid the entire amount before they unloaded the truck , even though they saw with their visible eyes that I had the cashier's check. I ask them, *" how I will know that you will go back and get the rest of my belongings now that you have been paid?"* The movers said you "won't know", trying to be smart. I was so angry, that I began to cry. All of a sudden I remember what my step dad had taught me growing up, and that was how to *"cuss"*. My step dad spoke French and English and he could call you some names that the *"cussing sailors"* did not have in their vocabulary. In the mist of all the anger and tears, Rita, said a *"bad word"*! My sister looked at me like I had lost my mind! She knows that I don't *"cuss."* Her look said, *"who is this so called Christian woman who just said a "bad word".* I cussed and asked God to calm me down in the same breath. Thank God for answered prayers. I am so glad that God heard my cry and the *Holy Spirit* calmed me down, because it was about to be *"on"* like *"donkey-kong"*! I don't know what your relationship with God is like, but I know, and God knows that if He don't calm me down right away, I will *"get out of the box."* I could not wait until I got home and ask God to forgive me for "cussing." I needed God to step in right away and control ME, *right then* and *right there!* I called the police to settle this matter and they said they could not force the company to unload my furniture, this was a matter for the court system. In the end I paid the company before they picked up all my furniture and brought it to the storage unit. I told the drivers that I was not pleased with their decisions and they could see that I was still very angry. I also told them they if they drove off with my money, that I would drive to New Orleans and find each one of them and kill all of them. I *"would pick them off like flies on a firing range."* Please remember, God is still working on me! I only said *"one bad word."* How many have your said recently?

As women of God, ask yourself, " is my speech Godly and pleasing to God?" If you feel your speech is not Godly and has not been pleasing to God, ask God to forgive you and sin no more. We should try to speak more of God, less of ourselves and our personal business, and have no provocative conversations!

HEAVEN HELP MY TONGUE

My tongue can be a weapon, I can build up or destroy.
Sometimes I say things, I don't really enjoy.

Don't bring me no nonsense or any foolish talk.
I'm trying to walk like Jesus,
and walk the walk He walked.

Being a Christian is not easy, I found out the other day,
When that woman called me a dirty name,
God said "Just walk away."

by
Rita J. Rushing

Chapter 8

THE REHAB COUNSELOR

(Practicing Without a License)

Anyone who is addicted to any type of substance is not of him or herself. It is clear there is another element working that is not of God. It is God's will that we be of sound mind and body without addictions. When the enemy enters into our lives, we must have someone cast out those demons. Some people are gifted to cast out demons. If you are not gifted to cast out demons, then you *"best"* leave it in the hands of those who are called and equipped by God.

Some of you have met men and are involved with men with serious issues. Issues such as drugs, alcohol, pornography, criminal activity and etc. You may feel that you can *rehabilitate* this man in to becoming the man that God's want him. Trust me, you are not equipped! You may say that his problem is psychological because he had a *"hard life"* growing up. Maybe his ex-wife took all of his money, and kicked him out. Or perhaps *"no good"* women in his past broke him down. You may also feel that you can cure him because he is open with you about his life. You knew this man had a problem when you met him and you saw all the red flags, but no, you are the *rehab counselor.* My question to you is, *"what institution of higher learning did you receive your doctoral degree in psychology?" " How many clinical trials have you observed in dealing with individuals who are substance abusers or engage in criminal behavior?"* If you have answered *"none"* to any of these questions, then you are *"out of your league!"* You not *qualified* to help this man. Leave all of the rehabilitation to the professionals who are able to help this man. If you really want to help him, pray for him from a far, and wish him well. Don't bring the drama and issues into your life or your home!

Some of these issues and problems are *demonically linked*. I don't know if you know this but, when someone become romantically involved with individuals who are possessed by demons, those demons can be transferred. It is called, *"the transferring of spirits."* Demons spirits never travel alone, there is always more than one demon. Remember the man who was living in the land of Gerasenes/Gadarenes who was possessed by demons? This man was paranoid and screaming because he was being tormented by demons day and night. When Jesus saw the man, the Word of God says in **Mark 5:8-13**, *For Jesus had already said to the spirit. "Come out of the man, you evil spirit." Then Jesus asked, "What is your name?" And the spirit replied, "Legion, because there are <u>many</u> of us inside this man." Then the spirits begged him again and again not to send them to some distance place. There happened to be a large herd of pigs feeding on the hillside nearby. "Send us into those pigs," the evil spirits begged. Jesus gave them permission. So the evil spirits come out of the man and entered the pigs, and the entire herd of two thousands pigs plunged down the steep hillside into the lake, where they drowned."* According to Roman military, during biblical times, a *"legion"* was the largest army unit that consisted of 3,000 to 12,000 of soldiers.

There are men and women of God today who are able to cast out demons and deliver person from possession of demons. Notice Jesus not only casted out the demons, but He also told the demons where to go. When men and women cast out demons they must tell those demons where to go, and command them not to come back. These people must be specific by telling those demons to go back to the *"pits of hell"* where they came from. If they *do not* specify where they should go, then they may come out of that person and perhaps into you, if you are in the room of deliverance. I suggest you step out of the *"line of fire"* in your so call *"rehabilitation."* Leave the deliverance or casting out demons to those persons that God has *"equipped"* for such a task of deliverance.

If you are involved in practicing without a license trying to get that man to stop using drugs, or stop drinking maybe this book will help you. The thing you must do is to *"turn in your license"* and stop your practice! My time is too valuable to waste, trying to get someone off something that he enjoying doing in the first place. If you are not careful, you will eventually need counseling yourself. For me personally, I will not become involved with a man who is on drugs or has an alcohol problem. The only *drink* that I want a man of mine to take regularly, is a *drink* from a *communion cup* when he takes the Lord Supper!

REHAB COUNSELOR

WHILE WALKING DOWN THE STREET ONE DAY
I SAW A MAN I KNEW,
HE SAID I KNOW YOU DONT REMEMBER ME,
BUT I REMEMBER YOU.

BUT THEN I REALIZED,
I REMEMBER HIM FROM SCHOOL,
AND FROM THE LOOKS OF THINGS,
HE HAD BEEN EATING DIRT OFF "THAT SPOON."

HE SAID LETS HAVE DINNER OR MAYBE A MOVIE OR TWO,
THEN I BEGIN TO WONDER, WHAT HE HAD BEEN GOING
THROUGH.

I AGREED TO HAVE DINNER EVEN THOUGH DOUBT ENTERED
MY MIND,
HE TOLD ME HIS LIFE STORY AND I EVEN SHARED MINE.

HE SAID HIS MAMA BEAT HIM AND HIS DADDY WENT AWAY.
I SAID, "POOR LITTLE THING, YOU HAD IT HARD ALONG YOUR
WAY."
HE SAID I NEED A GOOD WOMAN TO STAND BY MY SIDE,
HE SAID "I'M A GOOD MAN" AND SAID IT WITH PRIDE.

AS DAYS AND WEEKS AND MONTHS WENT BY HE BEGIN TO
CHANGE,
FOR NOW THE POOR LITTLE SCHOOL BOY IS NO LONGER THE
SAME.
I SOON FOUND OUT LATER THAT I WAS RIGHT ABOUT THE
"SPOON."
HE CAME TO MY HOUSE ONE DAY, HIGHER THAN THE MOON.

I ALLOWED THIS MAN TO ENTER MY LIFE BECAUSE I THOUGH I
COULD SET HIM FREE,
BUT NOW THE ONE IN NEED OF HELP . . . . IS ME!

BY
Rita J. Rushing and Kaylo L. Henry

Chapter 9

DRAMA, DRAMA, AND MORE DRAMA

The television set can be a very knowledgeable and useful tool for learning purposes. This tool is used to share with people who are interested in events around the world. We are able to view all types of programs for our enjoyment. There are programs that are so real, you would think that Victor Newman was really rich and still marry to Nikki. We call these programs soap operas, but in actuality they are programs that shows drama. But I found out over the years that kind of drama can be addictive. Silly me! However, I am proud to say that I am *no longer* addictive to that mess!

You may say that you are not into soap operas or that kind of drama. Perhaps you may have a little drama going on in your own life. You know exactly what I am talking about! I'm talking about drama in arguments, fighting, cussing, or like the old people use to say, *"just acting a fool."* When women get angry, we get angry! We don't care what we say, what we do, or who we hurt. We just want to be heard, taken seriously and *at times*, get even! If women would *look* at the man they are involved with, and how they got into the relationship in the first place, they will understand my point.

Everybody have a past and bless God we all have a future. When I say having a past, that means everyone have past relationships that include previous boyfriends, husband's girlfriends, and wives. When men and women don't take the time to investigate that new person in their lives it can lead to a whole lot of drama. Investigation takes an effort on one person's part to check out that person's background. You should want to know how his last relationship ended and what kind of drama was in that relationship. When women investigate they should check to see if there was any violence in that last relationship. Especially if there is any "*baby's mama drama.*" The reason I mentioned this is because some men have not ended the last relationship with the baby's mama. If it is not baby's mama, he is still seeing his last woman behind your back trying to make her jealous with his you!

You need to know whether or not the last woman he was involved with was violent and whether or not she had every been incarcerated. If she has been incarcerated for simple battery or domestic violence, because trust me, she don't mind going back to jail! Also, why you are checking backgrounds, see if he has every been incarcerated for any crimes, whether it's driving drunk, drug possession, rape, murder or etc. If you know he has been in *"trouble with the law"* then you need to dump him right away, because he don't mind going back to jail either.

I am reminded of an incident where a woman was involved with a man who had been involved in domestic violence with a previous girlfriend. The woman was aware of this man's background, in that he went to prison and served over ten years for shooting his last girlfriend. She also knew that he had a history of domestic violence with other women and was now beating her. She continued to put up with him and the drama he brought into her life. Her parents and family members try to warn her to stay away from this man and not to become involved with him, but she didn't listen. The Word of God talks about the importance of listening in **Proverbs 2:5,** "*A wise man will hear, and will increase learning; and a man of understanding shall attain unto wise counsels.*" Whether we choose to believe it or not, our parents always know best. One day the drama escalated, and this man shot and wounded her, killed her parents and other family members living in that household. This could have been avoided if she had just listened to her parents. She has to live with the fact that her lover killed her parents and other family members because of her failure to end that relationship! **Silly woman!**

I have heard some women say that all men lie, but I don't believe that at all. However, there are some men that lie and are still lying to you, even to this day. Don't think you are an *exception*, because you're not. One way to catch a lie is to be a good listener. Now listen to me! Okay? If you would listen you can catch a liar, if *you don't* <u>act so silly</u> *and stop all that giggling and showing your "teeth" when he is talking to you.* When I say silly, I mean talking all over yourself and not actually listening to what *he* is saying. Also be aware of his body language. If you continue to observe him and listen to what he is saying, you will eventually know whether or not he is telling the truth. But some women don't use this information to their advantage. Instead they are too busy " *looking up in his face"* for acceptance. You have accepted this man even though your observation of him indicated *"red flags."*

Now that you have a liar in your mist, you start lying as well. You lie to your family and friends and try to make people think that is just *wonderful* and the best thing since *"slice bread."* You start lying about his income and just how supportive he is to you. You know that man has not worked in five months, yet you claim he is at work when someone asks about him. Why do you *lie* for a *liar?* You know that he is not working, but you will lie to others to make him *look good* to others. You also lie because you don't want to look *bad as the person* who *"chose"* that man! You know that you are the person who is actually taking care of him. You provide free food, room and board and other amenities that come along with serving a *master.* He probably does not give you enough money to *"feed the birds perched in the tree"* or the *"cats in the yard."* I have not always been saved, but when I wasn't saved I did not put up with taking care of a man, nor did I want to be with a broke man! I felt at the time I was already *half broke,* what did I want with a man that was *completely broke.!* We would never have enough money to do anything or go anyplace. Then he would be *"looking up in my face."* He knows that I am *"half-broke"* with some money, and he is *"completely broke"* with <u>no</u> money. What are you looking at me for? You want me to pay for everything? You are the man, you should be taking me places!

I can say over the years that I have had some habits, but taking care of a man was never one of them! The Word of God tells us about work habits as indicated in **I Thessalonians 3:10, "**. . . *that if any would <u>not</u> work, neither should he eat."* I am <u>not</u> one of those Christians that believe some of the Scriptures in the Bible, I believe all of them. The Word of God says that if you don't work, you don't eat! As for me and my house . . ."*if you don't work, you don't eat!"* If you feel the need to take care of someone, you should take in a homeless woman and give her free lodging for a few months in order to get back on her feet. As far as taking care of him, tell him the Salvation Army provides food and lodging for persons who are jobless and penniless. However, the Salvation Army does charge a small fee as well. Don't forget to tell him you will pray for him and bid him Godspeed! That means may God be with you on your journey!

Physical and Emotional abuse are real and the affects can be long lasting and sometimes deadly. The first thing that needs to be addressed is the fact that <u>abuse</u> is present in the relationship. So often women of God *don't* and *won't* talk about this abuse. Instead they try and cover up the abuse by trying to *justify, explain, and defend* the actions of the men in their lives. The physical abuse are often times visible by some type of bruise or injury. The bruise mostly noted is a *"black eye."* I never in my life had a black eye, but if I did, I could only pray for the one that gave it to me. My prayer would be, *"Oh Lord, please help me from killing this person.!"* Being in a physical abused relationship is living a life of hell. The person being abused never know when the *"lick"* is going to come and what amount of force will come with that lick! I have heard about women remaining in relationships with violent men who have broken their ribs, arms and every other body part that God created in their bodies. Yet, they remain in the abuse.

Emotional abuse can be just as bad as physical abuse. Emotions are very high among women, because we are attracted to what we are told. When someone is emotionally abusive they know just what to say in order to push your buttons. What that person says maybe mere *"words"* but those words can *"cut"* like a knife. When people intend to hurt you they will use words to cut you like a knife. If someone loves you they will not use words to hurt you. You know the words I am talking about! When someone *"cusses"* you out, or talk to you like you are *"nothing,"* you must feel something by those words. I know that must hurt! But let me share this with you. You don't have to take that abuse. I have been in the grocery store and heard men *cussing women out* about food that she was buying with her *"food stamp card."* He's upset because he wants rib eye's and she's buying pork chops. What kind of foolishness is that! First of all, did he bring any rib eye money with him? Secondly, she is *"silly"* for feeding him with food stamps meant for her and her children! You don't have a *"thing"* and yet you have the nerve to be choosey! Help me today Lord!

I can't stand to hear people talk to people *"any kind of way,"* and as for me personally, you *will not talk* to me any kind of way. I remember long ago when I worked for a telecommunication company, my supervisor tried to talk to me any kind of way. I received permission from another one of my supervisors to go into another part of the building. The supervisor tried to *"show off"* in the presence of other supervisors. When I stepped into a room where she and the others were, she said, *"where are you going.?"* The way she said was very nasty! So, I turned around to see who she was talking to that was behind me. I knew she was not talking to me! When I looked behind me, I didn't see anyone. I said to her, "who *you* talking too?" She said I'm talking to you! I answered her question as to where I was going, because she was one of my supervisors. There was another person with me at the time, and the person said to me, *"Ms. Rita, I know you are angry. I can see the steam coming out of you."* I said, " you are absolutely right! I said to him, " *I can tell you one thing, before this day is over she will . . . . see me!"*. I went back to my seat and told the supervisor who had given me permission what happened. She knew the supervisor was wrong as well. I told her these words, "tell her I want to see her before I leave THIS DAY!" That supervisor avoided me the remainder of that day. At the end of the day, I searched all the buildings until I found her. I said to her, *"I need to talk to you!"* I told her that I had been given permission by another supervisor to go in another part of the building and I did not appreciate the way she spoke to me. I told her that I gave her the utmost respect as my supervisor and I expected the same in return. I went a bit further and told her, *"as long as I am here working on this job, YOU WILL not speak to me in that manner ever again!"* She could tell that I meant business. She could also tell that if she talked to me that way again, I was going to *"snatch"* her by her throat! That was the last time she spoke to me in that manner. One month later she fired me. I can tell you I never *"missed a beat"* after I was fired. The Lord sustained me. I did not see *not one* hungry day, and I am still in the same house that I own during that time. One year, to the date after she fired me, she was fired! She had just bought a house, the same month she was fired! What goes around, comes around! Don't ever come up against God's children! When you mess with me, you mess with my Daddy!

Single church going women will not talk to their pastors about being abused. They are afraid the pastor will ask if they are intimate with that person. She knows that if she admits to having sex, she will be told to stop having sex with that person. She does not want to stop seeing the man because he keeps her for being lonely. And she does *not* want to close her legs because he *"scratches"* that itch she has! In order to stop the abuse, you must stop having sex and being in the company of the enemy.

When a person tries to justify another person actions, they are really trying to declare the person to be *"blame free"*. When a woman is abused she will try to create a story line of incidents where as the man is blame free. I have heard stories like, *" he drank too much and that's why he . . ."* or *" it's my fault I pissed him off."* If you are with a man who *cannot control* himself then maybe you don't need to be with him at all. Maybe you should check yourself!

Explanation and justification go hand and hand. Explanation goes into greater detail and the story line becomes greater. The characters can include you, your family, his job, the church, and childhood memories. Most folks are tired of hearing excuses like, *"he's like that because his daddy left him and his family when he was a child, or his mama was sleeping with the deacon in the church and the pastor knew about it, and did nothing."* The explanation that I love the most is *"he wasn't like that when I first met him."* You start to blame everyone that he has ever been in contact with for *his* drama. "Well, you know he wasn't like that until he starting hanging around his Uncle Lester." Don't blame Uncle Lester for his personality changes. I believe it was always in him to change, you just ignored the red flags. He blames Uncle Lester and so do you. *He may **not have** been like that before Uncle Lester, but you see what he is like now and you're still with him!* Woman, please! Give us a break! Tell him to go and stay with Uncle Lester and leave you alone!

Every man wants a good woman to stand by him, but women go too far when they *defend or remain* in an abusive relationship. The sad thing is, many of these women *are not* aware they are *defending* these men in these relationships. There is no justifying, explaining or defense that can be made for someone who is not *worthy* of your love and affection. I am more than sure that other women of God have tried to convince you to come out of that abuse. For some reason you *have not* and *will not listen* to sound counsel. It's not that people are *"dipping in your business"* or *"may be jealous of you."* It is not because another woman wants your man for herself. None of those are the reasons folk are trying to convince you to come out of the abuse. Those people just want you to be <u>safe, alive, happy and able to do the Lord's work</u>.

Women usually take offense to those who have advised them to get out of the relationship. Don't be offended, but listen to what is being said to you. Maybe the person giving you the advice has been down that road before. Or perhaps God maybe using that person to speak wisdom into your life. The advice that is being given to you can be *wise* thought and you may learn something. The Word of God says in **Proverbs 4:11,** ***"I will teach you wisdom's ways and lead you in straights paths."*** Think about what is going on in your life and seek freedom from the abuse. Take the advice you are being given, and ask God to restore back to you all of your outer and inner beauty.

When someone gives you advice make sure that the advice is positive. Above all things, you should ***pray*** about ***all*** the advice you are given. There are people who call me and ask for my advice on certain issues in their lives. And I tell them these words, *" Remember, you called me, I did not call you. I was minding my own business and you asked me, right?! Don't expect me to say what you want to hear."* At that time, I am giving that person an opportunity to keep their business to themselves and cancel that call. It is not always the case that people *ask me* for advice. I give it willingly if I think it will help the situation. I have ask God to help me to keep my personal thought to myself with other folk business. God is still *"working on me"*. Sometimes I say things to people that can come across the wrong way and seem heartless. I remember one of my girlfriends said, *" Rita, you say anything to people!"* That bothered me when she said that to me. So that night I went before God and prayed and said *"God do I say anything to people?"* God said to me *"don't let nobody tell you about your mouth . . . for I*

(God) have a purpose for that." I didn't understand what God meant at that time, but what I felt deep down inside of me was that God was going to use my mouth for His purpose. Little did I know that I would be writing this book and saying things that some folk *dare not* say. This is why it is so important to go before God when people say things to us. The very thing that may be viewed as ugly to some can be used by God for his purpose. Even though my friend was criticizing the way I spoke to her, this is what she felt about me. God corrects his children and sometimes that correction may come through someone else. If I was wrong, I sought God for His answer. I *am not* above reproach and can be corrected. Keep in mind we are not like the people of the world who at times cannot receive constructive criticism. The Word of God talks about criticism in **Proverbs 12:16-18** " *a wise person stays calm when insulted. An honest witness tells the truth; a false witness tells lies. Some people make cutting remarks, but the word of the wise brings healing.*" I know that it is painful to hear the truth about the one that we love and ourselves. But it is even worse to carry on in that relationship and be a called a "*silly woman.*"

SHACKING INSTEAD OF PACKING

When I first met him, and looked into his eyes,
I knew in an instant I wanted to be his bride.

As years went by, each year I would say "it's in June,"
When I spoke to him about marriage, he would stare at the moon.

The shacking we started kept me on my back,
After all those years, I am ready to pack.

Packing is not easy, because there is always hope,
We don't have to have a big wedding, we can always elope!

But here I am shacking without any rings,
shacking without marriage is just some of the things.

Now my bags are packed and I am headed for the door.
with God as my guide, I will shack no more!

by
Rita J. Rushing

Chapter 10

SEX AND SOUL TIES

Over the last ten years, the attitudes of single women have changed. Years ago, single women would say they are *single, independent* and <u>not looking</u> for a man. Today, some single women are proclaiming they are *single,* and *looking* for a *good* man! <u>Very few single women ever proclaim they are single and waiting on God to send them their man.</u> To make such a proclamation means that God will be the *one* who decides who will be their spouse. Very few single women have given God *full authority* and *control* to make that decision in their lives. Many may claim to be waiting on God to send them their spouses, but the question is *"what are they doing with their bodies until God sends them their husbands?"* Are single women involved in relationships <u>without sex</u> or is <u>sex a part</u> of that relationship?

When we think of intimacy, what is the first thing that comes to your mind? For some women, it may be kissing, holding hands, and for others it may be foreplay. But for the majority of women, intimacy means having sex. Sex is often used as a substitute to fill a void in one's life or it can be used to show love in a committed relationship made to another in the sight of God. Single women who are allowing *someone* or *something* to bring them pleasure should rethink their decisions for self-gratification. Being vulnerable to the flesh will allow men to come to your aid for *your* gratification. It is obvious to a man that you wish to be viewed as sexy by the way you dress. Perhaps you have mentioned in your conversation with him, that you have not had sex in a long time, or the sex was not satisfying.

Now that you have made it known to him that you want to have sex or you have not had *"good"* sex in a while, he feels it is his *job* to bring you sexual fulfillment. Once you tell a man that you have not had sex or you are not happy with your partner you open up a *"can of worms."* This *"nut"* will say something like, *"I can make you feel good, or I can make you feel like a real woman is suppose to feel."* How does a *man* know how a real woman is supposed to feel? *This conversation is a conversation that should not take place in the first place!* But since you have opened up that *"can of worms"*, let's open it up! This man is now ready to prove to you what a great lover he is, and he is willing to pull out all of *"his tricks"* on YOUR back!

Kissing is always a great start for any sexual act. He already knows that kissing on the *lips* is only the *beginning* of this scenario. He already has plans for his *lips and its final destination on your body.* He is willing to go all the way kissing all the parts of your body from your head to your toe. *When I say every part of your body, I mean every . . . . part of your body!* Women of the world love those kinds of moving lips. Even women of God find this sexual act pleasurable and exciting, but hold that thought. Now since you are all heated up, where is God in all of this? God is nowhere in that sexual act even if it is your husband!

Women and men can have very perverted appetites, that included both oral and anal sex. The animals that God created do not have such appetites as that of humans. Animals do not perform such sexual acts with their mates, nor will they allow any other any animal to do so. Even the animals know when they have gone too far! But yet there are single women of God who are performing oral sex and allowing someone to perform anal sex on her. Everyone reading this book has been constipated at some time or another in their life. Constipation is painful and can cause discomfort. The pain and discomfort of constipation has caused drug manufactures to come up with drugs such as Metamucil or Dulcolax to help relieve such discomfort. Do you think that I would allow *any man* to penetrate me in my rectum for his satisfaction; I don't think so! Why in the world would a woman allow a man to constipate her bowels for his satisfaction? Oh my God! If God has blessed you to be *regular* without having to take drugs, why would you allow someone to cause you to be constipated and run the risk of damaging your rectum? God's creatures *do not* perform such unnatural sex acts and we can learn a lot from God's creatures about sex. If the animals are not performing such unnatural, acts, maybe we should rethink our actions be as well.

As I stated before *"staying on your back"* can cause spiritual regression if sex is used as a bargaining tool. When I say using sex as a bargaining tool, it means to use sex as a means to acquire favors, money or objects for self gain. Women know that a man is a sexual being with a high sex drive. Some women use this to their advantage to get what they want, especially if they know the man is inadequate or has a sexual dysfunction, or if he is *"too hot to trot"*. Women play games to get what they want from men. Older men act like fools when it comes to sexy provocative women, or women who will play with these *"old men"* in general. These women will go out and meet these men, and allow those men to touch their breast or fondle them in other places for that *"all mighty dollar"*. These women already know those *"old geezers"* cannot perform and they use that to their advantage. I met a woman years ago that had a *"sugar daddy."* She would call him when she needed money and the two of them would engage in a sexual act. When she told me how old he was I knew *he* couldn't do *"nothing"*, being in his late seventies and her in twenties. She told me that she would go to his office and he would fondle her breast for about ten minutes and he would give her one hundred dollars. She would tell how he would be moaning and groaning. I would laugh so hard until I cried. I thought that was so funny, I was very young at that time. Little did I know at the time, she was prostituting herself. Although she was not having *"straight sex"*, she was allowing him to fondle her breast for cash money. The sad thing about that relationship is that he was a pastor of a *"whole church"* with over five hundred members. Dear Lord, help us!

Today single women of God are still doing the same thing, allowing men to touch them here and stroke them there. Not only are women of God playing the touching game, they are also performing private dancing for men. Trust me I know, for I was once a private dancer for my ex—husband. I took pride in dancing and the art of the dance. It would drive my ex-husband crazy. I had the body moves, the lingerie, the high heels and everything to go along with the dance. The sad thing about the dancing was, I didn't want to stop dancing after we got a divorce. The next relationship I became involved in I danced in that relationship as well. I knew that if it worked on my ex-husband, it would work on this man as well. *I danced so well that I had them calling their **own** name!* But I thank God I am no longer a *"private dancer."* I am celibate, and have been for over the last *ten years*. I hung up my dancing shoes and I no longer have the desire to have sex without the benefit of marriage. Now when God sends me my husband . . . . we shall see!

Today women are dancing for all audiences both *men* and *women*. *I call it dancing for the devil.* Instead of these people going to strip clubs the women are dancing for their audiences in the privacy of their homes or etc. People get turned on to what they see, especially when they can reach out and touch it. There is nothing wrong with dancing for your husband, as a matter of fact, Solomon's, wife the Shulamite woman danced for him in **Song of Solomon in 6: 8-10** and Solomon was welled pleased. Some people say that the Shulamite woman didn't actually dance for Solomon, and that is debatable. But I do say that if you are moving your body in a provocative way, save those moves for your husband on your wedding night and the nights thereafter.

Lonely women often become involved in relationships for companionship and it usually ends up becoming sexual in the long run. Some single women of God *may not* have a steady relationship with a man. However, they will keep a man on the back burner to be intimate with on occasions. He is the man the neighbors will see coming in and out of her house on occasions. He is the one the nosey neighbors will see after dark going in and coming out. He is the same man that will take her to social functions. He will be there for her, he is her *"special friend."* One day she will have to pay her special friend for his companionship with intimacy. There are very prominent people in your church or community who have what they call a *"special friend."* When women make reference to that person being a *"special friend"* he is usually the person she is having sex with. I have always said that companionships come with a price. Soon or a later that man will ask you for something that he knows you have, and you will have to *"pay the piper."* Well you may say you don't have a special male friend, but what about that *"special friend"* you keep in your closet, or in your night stand? ***I am talking about the one that uses the Everyready batteries!*** I have heard of single women of God that have purchased sex toys for sexual gratification and as a matter of fact I know of some women personally. But I say *no* to sex toys! If she keep using her toy, she won't have a need for a man, and that is not God's way for us. God wants to send your husband to you so you won't have to bring pleasure to yourself. Keep your hormones in tack and allow your husband to bring forth all of the joy and pleasure you have stored up in you for him.

I have heard women say they during the late night hours is when they feel most sexual or when they want to have sex. These feeling occurs more frequently, especially on the weekends when their bodies are well rested from a week of hard work. It is often during the wee hours or late night hours when women will allow men to make a *"booty call"* or the women themselves. There is no commitment, no exchange of small talk or a meal; it is just what it is, a *"booty call."* These so called *"booty calls"* are actually calls of desperation by one or both parties. But let me tell you what to do when that call comes through. Don't answer the telephone, or the door. And if you are the one who is leaving your house to go and make the *"booty call"*, I say fall on your knees and pray. Simply call "1-800—J-E-S-U-S. All lines are available and operators are standing by, ready to take your call!

For single women of God, sex can be a *killer.* It can be a killer if you are having sex with someone and you are not married to that person, according to the law and in the sight of God. The Word of God says in **Hebrews 13:4** *"Marriage is honorable among all, and the bed is undefiled; but fornicators and adulterers God will judge."* God is *not* pleased when we have sex outside of marriage, and having sex outside of marriage can have an adverse affect on you. The most adverse affect it will have on you, will be how it affects your relationship with God. It will slowly kill the relationship you have with Him! The Word of God tells us about sexual sin and gives us instruction on how to handle sexual sin. It states in **I. Corinthians 6: 18-20,** *"Run away from sexual sin. No other sin so clearly affects the body as this one does. For sexual immorality is a sin against your own body. Or don't you know that your body is the temple of the Holy Spirit, who lives in you and was given to you by God! You do not belong to yourself, for God bought you with a high price. So you must honor God with your body."*

It is not that God doesn't want women of God to have sex; it only becomes a problem with God if a woman is having sex outside of the bond of *"holy matrimony."* God is delighted when women of God have sex with their spouses for reproduction, bonding love and overall enjoyment between husbands and wives. Don't allow sex outside of marriage to put a wedge between you and God or tarnish your relationship with God. Walk away from fornication and walk with God because He already knows what you have desire of before you ask. Pray and ask God to let your sexual desires lie dormant until God sends your husband to you to stir up your desires on your wedding night. This is not a hard thing to do, but most women are not willing to ask God to do such a task. The reason is, because they want to continue to have sex. But I can only imagine what joy and fulfillment awaits for all of us who are single women of God. God will be pleased when the fire is rekindled on that special night. When God sends your husband you can ask God to help you bring pleasure to your husband. We know that God always sends help, even in the bedroom! So save your desires for your husband. Save those, *" I love you"* for him and him only. Tell him you love him often, and he will tell you and show you how much he loves you as well.

There are three little words that is understood and recognized around the world, and those words are, *"I love you."* Those three little words can get a woman into the bedroom, even if she has made a commitment to God to stay out of the bedroom. Most people used those words to convey or express to another person what they are actually feeling or to gain sexual favors. It is also words that can be used in a manipulative manner in order to receive something from another person. Some women have waited all their lives to hear those three little words. There are also other words that are used by some to express a deeper feeling or connection with another; and that word is *"soul mate."*

For many years I have often heard people claim another human as being their *"soul mate."* I too am guilty of having made such foolish statements as to claim someone as my *"soul mate"*. Silly, silly me! People often use terms and make proclamations of things they don't have a clue as to what they are saying, especially as Christians. These proclamations and behaviors don't line up with the Word of God. ***They should not be used in order to express our affection for another human being.*** Women of God are currently using worldly terms like other women who are not saved to express a stronger and deeper love for a man. These women want these men to know that they're love has gone **deeper** than the heart, it has **surpassed** the heart and now have **reached** their soul. *But let me say to all of those women who are giving their souls to another human being. **God has not, nor has He created another human being to be a part of another human being soul!** God created us to praise, worship and have fellowship with Him. He created us for Himself and we belong to Him. We do not have the authority, nor have we been given permission to give something away that belongs to Him (God).*

God created us in a human form and we are a three part beings: *spirit, soul, and body.* The *spirit* is the part of us that *communicates* with God, the *soul* is the part of us that *controls* **our mind, will and emotions**, and the *body* is the part that **houses our organs.**

The spirit is *unable* to control the soul and the body on its own. The **spirit** (communication with God) has to be fed in order to be strong and remain strong. We feed our **spirit** when must pray, meditate, worship, praise, and fast. We must also read and study our Bible and have fellowship with other believers. When we refuse to allow the **spirit** (God) to control our lives and the **soul** (mind, will and emotion) takes control, we become *carnal* or (allow the flesh to take control).

When the **soul** (mind, will and emotion) takes control, it will tell the **body** (our organs) what to do and when to do it. When this happens, the **soul** (mind, will and emotion) does what it wants to do, making sure that the **soul** (mind, will and emotion) is satisfied. The **body** (organs) has to do what is pleasing to the **soul** (mind, will and emotion).

While all of this is going on with the **soul** (mind, will and emotion), the **spirit** (God) is not in control. When this happens, God is not in any decisions we make! The **soul** (mind, will and emotion) and the **spirit** (God) should be on one accord or on the same page. When they are *not* on one accord then *carnality* (flesh) will step in.

Carnality occurs when someone physical needs, or appetites *(sex)* contrast with spiritual **(God)** qualities. The Word of God says in **Romans 8:7—8** " *the sinful mind is hostile to God. It does not submit to God's law, nor can it do so. Those controlled by the sinful nature cannot please God.* " Carnal

Christians are persons who go to church, and attend Bible study. They serve on usher board number one, two, three and sing in the choir. For some reason you <u>cannot</u> tell the difference between them and persons who are unsaved. Their behavior is the same as the unsaved. They visit the same places as the <u>unsaved,</u> display the same behavior as <u>unsaved</u> and bring reproach to the name of the God that created them. *However, they do obey some* of the instructions from God, but not all of the instructions from God.

This person is double minded, unstable and the weakness of their **soul** (mind, will and emotion) can be seen in their instability. The **spirit** (God) must be fed constantly. It is not enough just because you are saved. During salvation only the **spirit** (God) is sanctified or redeemed, not the **soul** (mind, will and emotion). The **soul** (mind, will and emotion) has to go through sanctification. This process is a continuous process that should *never* end. As we grow as Christians, we should learn the things that *are* of God and separate ourselves from the things that are *not* of God.

Now that we know about the **spirit, soul** and **body,** let's talk about a *"soul mate"*. Let me ask you this question, now that you have met this person are you ready and willing to give your *"soul"* to that person? What part of you are you reserving for God?

The Word of God says in **Mark 12:30,** *"You must love the Lord your God with all your <u>heart, all your soul, your entire mind and all your strength</u>."* When you give your **"soul"** to someone, then what part of your *"soul"* is left for God? You have openly confessed from your *own* mouth that you have given your *"soul"* to another human being, and that person is your *"soul mate"*. *When we give another human being any portion of our <u>" soul"</u> then he or she becomes our god!* Keep in mind whoever controls the **soul** (mind, will and emotion) *controls* the **body** (organs) and the **spirit** (God). When you give your soul to someone you are then *linked* up or *tied* to them in a relationship. The two of you are now linked and your *souls are tied* together.

Soul ties can be formed when someone worships another human being. Confession from our own mouth that we have given our *"soul"* to another person, is forbidden according to the Word of God. When people become linked together in a *"soul tied relationship"* their behavior can become extreme and demonic. Wild and crazy thoughts becomes embedded in their **soul** (mind, will and emotion). They will go as far as to commit murder, suicide or both in order to control or maintain whatever they feel belongs to them. When you find women who remain in a abusive relationships, there is a strong indication that *"soul ties"* are involved. People with common sense may not understand why a woman would remain in a relationship with a man who beats her severely. The reason she won't leave him is because this relationship is *bound up, unnatural* and *Satan* has her soul. Satan has the man bounded and because she has given her **soul** to that man, both *souls* now belong to Satan.

Soul relationships and any relationship where jealousy and controlling occurs are not of God. **It is a form of witchcraft.** Do you remember the story in The Word of God about Jezebel? The story of Jezebel can be found in **I Kings Chapters 21 verses 18—21.** Jezebel was a queen who was jealous, controlling and greedy. Jezebel wanted the land that belongs to Naboth, but Naboth would not sell the land to her. Jezebel wanted the land so bad that she gave a royal order to have Naboth killed in order to get the land. Naboth was stoned to death and Jezebel got her wish. She had so much control that she could issue an order to have him killed. Persons who are involved in witchcraft will try and use their devices to alter a person's mind, or get them to do something against their will. God is not against us loving another human being, but it is the way the way we love, and the way that we obtain that love that gets us into trouble.

Loving someone to the extreme can cost people their lives, and cause them to sin. I said from the beginning of this chapter that I too once claimed someone as my *"soul mate"*. I didn't know at the time, what I was saying and what part I was willing to give away to another. I thank God I know better, and the word *"soul mate"* is no longer a part of my vocabulary. Never again will I express to another human being that my *"soul"* is linked to that person. Now that I know I *cannot* continue to sin with my mouth and give someone a part of me that is reserved for God. The Word of God says in **Romans 6:1-2, and 6,** *"What shall we say then? Shall we continue in sin, that grace may abound? God forbid. How shall we, that are dead to sin, live any longer therein? Knowing this, that our old man is crucified with him, that the body of sin might be destroyed, that henceforth we should not serve sin."* Once I became knowledgeable of how I had sinned, I asked God for forgiveness. I told God that I was foolish and I vowed to never repeat those words again.

My soul is not mine to give, especially when I confess that I belong to God! And if God has not given any part of me away, I *do not have* the right, nor do I have the *authority* to give away any part of me that belongs to Him. I am still waiting on God to give *my hand* in marriage to another human being. And when God does sends me my mate for life, which will be my husband, my **soul** (mind, will and emotion) will still belong to God!

Chapter 11

WHO IS YOUR GOD?

Growing up in a single home today is almost the norm, and the parent of that single home is usually a woman. There are some women who are single, who will go to great lengths to prove to a man that she wants him and she is willing to go that extra mile. When I say extra mile, she will neglect her children, family, job, health, friendships and even her God to please him. I wish that someone could help me understand how some women can neglect their *God* and their *children* for the sake of a man.

I believe that God should always be the center of every Christians life, with family following. Children today have so much to content with and when the mother has issues of her own, it matriculates over to the child/children. Children are force to deal with problems at school, and then the child has to come home and deal with a mother who unhappy, neglectful and running behind a man! As soon as the child/children enter the home they can tell the mother is "*in rare form.*" Your children are able to see how your demeanor or mood changes when you are upset with a man. You become like Dr. Jekyll and Mr. Hyde, one minute your happy when you are around him, and depressed when you're not. Sometimes depression sets in so deep, you *cannot* and will not get out of bed. I say to shake yourself from this madness with this man, and come out of that depression that is affecting you and your children. Keep in mind when you are depressed or on "*the pity pot*" you *cannot* hear from God who is still on the throne. You are too engulfed in your own sorrow or pity to know that only God can give you the joy and peace that you so desperately seek.

When children are neglected it will appear in their behavior and learning abilities. In the case of young females, they become sexually active at a very young age. Those young girls start wearing those tight clothing, and *"switching"* like they are grown women. The parents of those young girls may think is okay, and some will make comments like, *"girl she got that shape on her, or . . . girl I was shaped like that when I was her age . . . . I was "fine" just like that."* When people began to talk about the way she walks the parent will say, *"girl I use to walk just like that.. or girl I use to "switch" just like that."* The next thing you know, she has *"switched"* herself upon a baby! But I ask you this question, *"where were you when she was wearing those tight fitting clothing?"* I know you saw her *"switching"* like she was a grown woman. Why didn't you stop her from all that *"switching?"* That young girl has *"switched"* upon something she cannot feed or clothe. Now you, the grandparent, has the responsible to feed one more mouth in the home. Oh by the way, don't expect any stable child support or income coming from the father of that child. You are now responsible for that *"switch,"* and that *"switch"* that was created by your daughter can *"holler"* all night long.

There are instances where women have neglected their children so much, that later in life the children put their parents in *"check."* When the children became adults themselves, they *"throw up"* in their parents faces the neglect they received as a child. The child/children will tell you all about Mr. Johnny, and how you put Mr. Johnny before them. They will speak of how <u>you allowed</u> Mr. Johnny to cuss them or punish them for no reason. They will tell you all about your past lovers and the neglect they received from them as well. Your children will remember Mr. Johnny because they believed he was the *"wedge"* that came between you and them. Although Mr. Johnny *may* have been the reason for some of the abuse and neglect, Mr. Johnny is <u>not there</u> to hear your children put you in *"check"*. The only way to solve this problem is to ask your children to forgive you for the neglect. You must *"own up"* to what you did to your child/children and take full responsibility. You must also ask God to forgive you, and ask God to give you wisdom in raising your child/children, so there won't ever be another, Mr. Johnny story!

All of us have jobs that we do, whether we work in the home or outside the home. Our jobs are important or should be important to us. Jobs are important because is the means in which we feed ourselves and our families. But if a woman is trying to hold on to a man she will risk her job to keep her hold. She is not concerned that she will be reprimanded for being late or suspended for a week or two. Forget about being placed on probation, *Sister girl* could care less!

We all know that we should report to work on time, and spend the time we are paid, doing our job. Some women spend a lot of valuable time at work trying to reach a man. They will spend all their time calling him trying to find out his location or *"texting"* someone about the issue she is having with that man. It is women like that which made companies state in their company's polices, *"no personal telephone calls on the job."* She has been on the telephone four out of the eight hours she was paid and she is still running her mouth. If she is not on the company telephone trying to save her "minutes", she is in the bathroom on her cell phone using her minutes. She is calling everywhere to find him or chase him down. Don't chase him, replace him. Honestly, if I have to keep up with a man like that, I don't need him.

Sleep is very important to me. So much so, I would rather sleep, then eat. I know that sounds crazy. Some women could care less about their sleep. Others try and make up for their lack of sleep, by taking a nap when they come home from work. Women say to their children, *"mama will feed you and check your home work after I take a little nap."* That nap may last two hours. The children are so hungry, they start cooking their own food! For those who cannot cook, they boil water in the microwave and open up a bag of Roni noodles. If she *does not* sleep too long she will wake up to feed her children, but the child/children will have to check <u>their</u> own homework. She has to make her call! If she cannot reach him, she starts cussing. She calls Mary and tells Mary that *"so in so"* has not called or came over. Mary adds her too cents, and says, *"girl I wouldn't take that if I was you . . . you need to get rid of him."* But I say, calm down, say your prayers and go to sleep! When God sends you a man you want lose sleep, neglect your children or *"cuss"* when he does not call or show up. God is going to make sure that man has respect for you and your children. He will not come to your home late at night or keep you out too late at night. He will be ever so mindful that you must get your *"beauty rest"* to continue to look good to for yourself and for him! Oh by the way! Stop telling Mary your business and starting talking to God about it. Mary *cannot* calm your nerves, she can only *aggravate* the situation. The **only one** that can calm you down, is the **Master** that calms the seas! Please remember that!

Women who desert their long time friends for a man can lose a precious friendship. When some women meet men they go berserk and forget all about their long time friendship, for the newly found friend. If that man says he does not like your long time friend, some women will give up their old friendship. She begin to avoid her old friend or pretend she is too busy to talk. But what she doesn't realize is that friend will be there for her when he is gone! The Word of God talked about the friendship that David had with Jonathan. In **I Samuel 18:1-4 . . . "And Jonathan made a special vow to be David's friend . . . ."** The thing that gets in the way of friendships is *"jealousy"* and the *"control factor"*. Jealousy can be a dividing force of that friendship if he is jealous of the *"closeness"* that you have with your girlfriend. When that man want you to spend more time with him, and less with others, the control factor is in place.

Any time he wants you to separate yourself from people you love and care about, you need to rethink about that relationship with him. Today he wants all of your time, next he is controlling your mind. Today it is the separation of family and friends, tomorrow is separation from God! Don't allow him to separate you from others, only to cling to him.

Who is God and how important is He to you? Any relationship you have *without* God being a part of it, is no relationship! Whether your role in that relationship is that of mother, sister, cousin, friend, lover or mate. With each relationship that you form, you should have a **greater** relationship with God! The bond you have with God *should be* so strong that you will not allow anyone to change, manipulate, or control you to the degree that you forget all about God. Always be mindful what God has done for you and brought you through. I have heard of women who stopped going to church all together because that man did not attend church. *What is wrong with you?* Don't you know that is the hand that Satan fan's? *Satan wants you to get with this man who is unsaved.* Then, Satan will have two people who have turned their back on God! **Let the heathen go!** Don't *you* turn your back on God.

One of the Ten Commandments written in the Word of God, in **Deuteronomy 5: 7 says,** *"Thou shalt have none other gods before me."* But for some reason some women have and are worshipping other gods. This god is not one that has many followers or worshippers, you may be the *only* worshipper of this god. Now if this man is seeing you and someone else who also think that he is a god, then maybe you're not alone! When a woman set up a man up or make him think he is a god, she will have to continue to bow down and please this *monster* she has created. This self made god is never happy, neither will he allow you to be happy. His demands will be great and you will have to continue to do everything that is pleasing to him. You will never have a day of rest from this god that you have created, it becomes a never ending saga! But let me remind you, even God rested according to the Word of God in the book of **Genesis 2: 2,** *" And on the seventh day God ended his work which He had made; and He rested on the seventh day from all his work which he had made."*

If God rested, when do you get your rest? This was your doing, so don't complain now! **You did this when you took God off the throne, and put this man on the throne!**

I know you are aware this relationship is not good for you. Perhaps you don't want to end the relationship because of the hurt and pain. But is okay to hurt when you end a relationship. It is even more difficult to end a relationship, when the woman has been running behind the man to capture him in the first place. Most breakups will result in the shedding of tears, heartache and a few sleepless nights. I know about this personally, I have been there and done that! These emotions are considered a norm in the breakup of any relationship. When those emotions go beyond a certain period of time, it becomes *unreasonable.* God sees and understands our pain, but when do we go on with our life? God spoke to the children of Israel after the death of Moses. The Israelites were moaning and groaning after the death of Moses, and they were at a standstill. The Word of God says in **Deuteronomy 34: 8** *"The people of Israel mourned for Moses on the plains of Moab for <u>thirty days</u>, until the customary period of mourning was over."* God saw their grief and felt their pain, and God allowed them to *"stay still"* for a period of **thirty days**. Now that you know God gave **His Chosen People** <u>thirty days </u>to mourn, why is it day **365** for you? You need to bury that issue and keep moving like the Israelites!

I remember once, and I did say, once! To me, once means one time! I remember *one* time I was in a relationship and that relationship ended. I was so hurt. I loved that man so deeply, that *I cried all night long after the breakup. When I say, all night long, I mean,* <u>all night long!</u> The next morning when I woke up and looked at myself in the mirror I was in shock. I did not recognize myself. My face was swollen and I could not see my eyes, only a part of my eyelids. *I looked like a big face black bear with no eyes*! I realized the reason I looked like a big face black bear was because I had cried all night long. **Then it hit me! I said, "oh my God!"** I dropped down immediately on my knees on my hard tile floors. I didn't think about the surface my knees would hit, I just knew that I had to drop down immediately before MY GOD.! I said, **"Lord I have cried all night long over this man like he is <u>my</u> God. Lord please forgive me for crying like a fool. <u>*Never again, oh Lord will I cry behind a man like he is my God*</u>. Lord it does not matter to me as to who comes, or who goes . . . . as long as you don't ever leave me, oh God! I thank you God for your forgiveness in Jesus Name, Amen!"** My tears ended that day! The God that I love and serve is a God of comfort and peace. God does not want me to continue to be hurt and foolish. Stop trying to hang on to that small and useless god that has no power other than to make a fool out of you. Let it go! When you make up in your mind to stop idolizing this man and let him go, God will be there to help you make the transition from being *"silly"* to being *"sensible.!"*

Let's talk about favors. What do you consider a favor? When someone asks me if I can do them a favor, before I answer yes, my response is *"it depends on the favor. "*Women who are committed to serving men whom they are *not* married to will jump before he could complete the question and answer yes! Most of the time the favor involves providing him with something that he would not ask of his mother or his sister. Such favors include doing his laundry, ironing his clothes, performing illicit acts during sex, and the big one of all, loaning or giving him money. My question for you is, "*who was doing his laundry before you met him, or who performed the illicit act before he met you."* Ask that man, "*where is your people, why are you asking me?"*

I believe the reason some men make such request of some women is because these women have a mark on their forehead that identifies them. That identity has the word "*fool*" written all over it. When a man knows how eager a woman is to please him, he knows she will *never* refuse him of anything! He knows that he has a "*all day sucker*" whom he can control and "*con*" to do just whatever he wants her to do! It is disgusting to see women go out on a limb and do all those things to please these men. Don't get me wrong, I am *not men* bashing because I love men too. *But don't go out on a limb, if that man is not your husband!* You should go out on a limb to help your husband, because after all the Word of God says in **Genesis 2:18** "*And the Lord God said, It is not good for man to be alone; I will make him a help meet for him."* God said to **help**, *not sponsor!* If you feel the need to sponsor someone, please sponsor a child! God intended for a woman to help the *husband* He has given you, not the man you are "*shacking with or playing house.."* As I said in the previous chapters, you should not be "*shaking or playing house"* in the first place. If you are playing wife, give up that title and via for the title of being "*holy".*

Money is something that everyone needs and some people have to work hard in order to make money. Some people have worked on jobs for years and still don't make enough money to run their household. To that person, loaning money to someone is liking slapping them in the face, because they cannot afford to loan money. Our mothers taught many of us to save some money for emergencies or for a "*rainy day."* It is a good thing to try and have a little something saved for emergencies, but what is considered an emergency. Do you consider it an emergency when you take the "*rainy day"* money to use as a down payment for him a car? Would you consider it an emergency to bail him out of jail? What about catching up on his back child support payments, or pay his attorney fees?

Well you may say, "*I don't give him or loan him any of my money for that"*, and that may be true. You still may be just as guilty in the favor department if you co-sign or establish an account in your name for his use. I am talking about getting a cellular telephone in your name that he will use. Or giving him a credit card or the use of your credit for him personally. But don't feel bad, you are not alone with this foolishness.

There are some women who operate a credit establishment in their own home, doing business as a loan company. This business, however *does* discriminate, because this woman only loans *her money* to men! You are probably thinking she has a surplus of resources or money to operate her business, but she doesn't. She operates by **"robbing Peter to give to Paul."** She is aware that the money she is loaning to him is needed to pay her utilities, mortgage, rent, car note, or feed her families. She is not concerned if the money she loaned him will be paid back on the date of agreement, or if he will pay it back at all. She knows the utility bill is past due and due by no later than Tuesday at the close of business day. But she is not worried. She *trusts* the borrower of the money. She does *not* believe the utility company will disconnect on Wednesday. She loves and trusts this man, and his word is good enough for her. So much so, she is willing to allow herself and her family to sleep in the dark if necessary. When her utilities are disconnected, she then calls all around town trying to get someone to pay her bill. She calls all the churches, community centers and community organizations. She calls the council person in her district to see if he could help. She also calls her family and friends for someone to *"help her"* get her utilities back on. She calls family and friends and gives them a sad story about not being able to pay her bill. Well you know Big Mama will go into her *"bosom"* and give you all of her emergency money, because she don't want to see those grandchildren in the dark. Let me ask you this! Did you tell Big Mama or anyone else that you had the money and loan it to that man? Did you tell her that? I don't think so!

There are lot of men who are as *"broke as Job's turkey"* whatever that means. However, women are willing to loan him money, knowing she will never see the money again. If the church is collecting money for a special fund, she is the same woman who is quick to say, *" oh I don't have no money, or she will pull out lose change to put in the basket"* But I wonder why she don't tell the man the same thing she tells the church, *"I don't have no money?"* Not only does she refuse to give on special Sunday's, or any church projects, but she refuses to give to God at all. Stop digging in your purse trying to muster up a few pennies to give to God! **When <u>you</u> <u>should</u> have been digging in your purse to give to that man, you weren't. The Word of God tells us in Psalm 54:6,** *"I will sacrifice a voluntary offering to thee: I will praise thy name, O Lord for it is good."* This means we should give out of a grateful heart because we are aware that God makes *all* that we <u>have</u> and <u>own</u> possible. Not only that but God loved us so much that he gave, not just money, but his only Son to redeem a lost world. And if you are living on planet Earth, that means you are included in that lost world. Stop worshipping this *"fake "*god and <u>worship only</u>, The True and Living God!

WHO SAID GOD WAS DEAD?

Who was it that started the rumor that God was dead?

Where did you get your information?

Was it from the "street committee" who never gets anything right?

Or from the people on the other side of the tracks?

Did you read it about His death in the classified?

Or was your source the Internet?

Those who worship idols says He's not real.
But those of us who know Him, says He's the real deal!

Who put that rumor out that God was dead?
Tell the devil's he's a liar
He watches us while we're in bed!

by
Rita J. Rushing

Chapter 12

MONEY, BODY AND TIME

I've heard some people say there is a shortage of men, while others will disagree and say there is no shortage of men, but a shortage of "good men." I don't believe there is a shortage of men, but I do agree there is a shortage of men of God. There are men everywhere, on every street corner, in the mall, and in the church. I am more than sure you have made this observation in your church or other churches. Single men in congregations stick out like a sore thumb, and even more so, if he has money. If there are single men in your congregation I am sure the women swarm around him likes bees to honey. Often times they will swarm in sets of three or more for his attention.

If a man shows an interest in a woman, sometimes the effects can be overwhelming. Her head will start to spin at though she had a drink of alcohol. Now she says to herself, " *he likes me.* " And then you start playing the guessing game within your mind as to try and figure out how much he likes you, or how often he thinks about you. Then you say to yourself *"if he's thinking about me, I must look good."* Now that he has shown an interest, the two of you exchange telephone numbers for future calls. So here we go!

Instead of some women of God waiting for the man to make the first move socially, she makes the first move and invites him to her house. She then decides to cook something special for him. Did he ask you to cook something special? Did he ask you to cook at all? These women of God will prepare seafood, rib eye's or sirloin steaks with all the fixings including dessert and set the table for dining. But I ask the question, *"For What?"* Because someone once said, *"the way to a man's heart was through his stomach."* Honey let me give you a news flash. *If this is the man that God has chosen to be your mate, you can serve him boil peanuts and he will still fall in love with you!* Forget about the expensive meals and save your money and your time. Some women of God are buying seafood, rib eye's and sirloin steaks for these men and probably **have never** served their *own children* such meals. If you are *not* one of these women you probably know a woman of God who does those things. They serve their children cereal and milk, hotdogs or pork and beans. The only time the children see the table set, with all the fixing is Thanksgiving or Christmas. Now that the meal has been served, she waits for a compliment. She hopes that he will say the meal was delicious or better yet, the best meal he has ever eaten. If he compliments the meal, she feels she has something to draw him to her, even if it means cooking him another meal.

A woman is one of God's most precious gems, yet some women allow themselves to be treated not as something precious, but a *common commodity.* Men are *allowed* to degrade some women, not merely alone, but with help from the *woman herself.* We fall in love head over heels at the drop of a man's hat. But the questions becomes, *"who are we in love with; is it him or is it Him?"* Some will give all of their love, time and money in a *hopeless* situation. If you look in your wallet or checkbook right now what would you do, laugh or cry? If you said laugh you probably have a few dollars, but if you said cry, you probably are broke! But the question is not whether your broke or have money, the question is, *"what are you willing to do, or who are you willing to sleep with in order to get money?"* What are you doing, or thinking about doing in order to pay your bills? As I stated previously, single women maintain most homes without an adequate income to provide for themselves or their children. They probably do what must most people do in similar situations, and that is *"rob Peter to pay Paul."*

Nobody likes the idea of not having enough money to make ends meet. It is not having a *lack* that corrupts women of God minds and bodies, it is what they will do to get the money that corrupts. There are women of God today who are *"sleeping with men"*, and *"shacking up"* in order to get money from these men. This also includes being with someone for the sake of money. It also means that you receive money or something that you want each time you sleep with him. It also includes *"holding out"* on sex if he does not give you want you want. I don't know what it sounds like to you, but it sounds like *prostitution!* I know there has to be some sort of *"exchange"* when he comes to your house so frequently. *I know that man is not staying overnight while the two of you shell peas in your bedroom!*

When folk here the word *"prostitution"* the first person they think about is the woman walking the streets. She is the one walking the streets, *"switching"* her body, often wearing provocative clothing. To some it may clear she is looking to sell her body for money. But what about the women who **do not** walk the streets like a *"street walker"* yet, they are sleeping with men for money. I talking about the women who have *"prostituting relationships"* with men in order to get money. There is only one difference between the two women. <u>One is walking the streets looking for men; the other use her telephone or make face-to-face contact to arrange her meeting.</u> Another factor is the *"street walker"* will exchange her body for money anywhere and anyplace, the other woman will use her home, or a motel or any place that is considered *"descent."* <u>We **cannot** look at the clothing or location of the "prostituting events," **we must look at what was exchanged!**</u> <u>In both cases it was sexual favors for money.</u> If you are sleeping with men for money or favors, that makes you a prostitute my dear!

Children are beautiful gifts from God, and these gifts imitate what they see you do in the home. Please don't tell me women of God that men are staying overnight or shacking when you have minor children in the home! This is definitely not good for you or your children. How do you expect your child/children to respect *you* when they see a man coming to your home and go in your bedroom? The children go to bed and wake up the next morning and he is still in house. Then the next day you want to play Betty Crocker and cook that *fabulous* breakfast for him and serve him breakfast in bed. Then you want to play it off like you cook such a breakfast all the time. You know that you have taught your children to go to the cupboard and get that box of cereal and you hope there is milk in the refrigerator.

Children in the home can see so much in their short childhood because of your *lack* of respect. Don't be surprised if your children start *disrespecting* you and going *"toe to toe"* with you in your conversation. When I say going toe to toe with you, I'm saying your child will start talking back to you as if he or she is the parent! What is sad women of God, your female children are going to grow up and do the same things you have done, having sex for money. They will shack themselves or become pregnant out of wedlock. Jesus mother, Mary was the only single woman who became pregnant through *"immaculate conception"* and this was the <u>only</u> pregnancy that pleased God. God is not pleased when young girls become pregnant before marriage. If these are some of the things that are going on in your home, you must cease with this behavior. The Word of God tells us in **Proverbs 22:6,** *"Train a child in the way he should go, and when he is old he will not turn from it."* You don't need to take this man's money and sleep with him, and you definite don't need to teach your children your *"old tricks"*.

As women of God we need to always *"check ourselves"*. Ask yourself, who you are and whose you are? If you say you are a child of the **Most High God** you don't have to go to mortal men like Kevin, Robert, James, or others to give you money. God is your source! The Word of God says in **Haggai 2:8, *"The silver is mine, and the gold is mine, says the Lord Almighty."*** If the gold and silver belongs to your Father who is in heaven, then why are you going to men who can go bankrupt at any given time? Oh by the way, the same thing goes for those who shack because you **cannot** afford to acquire a place and live on your own. Stop saying stupid stuff like *"Oh we don't sleep together, he sleeps in his bed and I sleep in mine."* I hope you know that you are the only person who believes that mess! I believe the only time two single people should live under the same roof is when they have heard from God. The two will be as roommates with no strings attached. Both parties should have the understanding that this is actually what it is, nothing more and nothing less! Make it perfectly clear, there will be no sex involved.

As women of God we have to put our faith and trust in God and not man to meet our needs. The reason you are struggling with paying your bills is because you don't trust God and you're not a *tither.* If you trusted God, there would be no need for you to rely on that man to help you pay your bills. When you rely on someone other than God to meet your needs, you are subjected to *"dance by their music"* and do what they say do. When that happens that means you must have sex with him. You must also perform other *"illicit acts" when* he wants it, *wherever* he wants it, and even if it's *all night* long. There is nothing wrong with having sex with your husband all night long if this is what you both want to do. But it becomes quite a *chore* when you must *"perform"* in order to pay a debt! *Jesus Christ died on the cross to pay my debts and I owe no man nothing but to love him with the love of the Lord!*

I know that you are probably struggling to make ends meet, but what do you do with the money you have? Do you pay your tithes or do you play the lottery, bingo, or just overall gamble with God's money? You may say, well *"I don't gamble, but if you're not paying tithes, yes you are gambling"*. Your gambling or taking a chance on the fact *whether* or not you will have enough money to pay your bills. If you are taking such a chance on your needs being met, then you are a **"silly"** woman. I remember when I worked for this agency and some of my co-workers would pool their money and buy lottery tickets. Because I was a new employee or the *"new kid"* on the block folk weren't sure whether or not I gambled. One day one of my co-workers came to me and asked whether or not I would be interested in putting money in the pot to buy lottery tickets. She informed me how it worked and she was ever so quick to announce that the group had won money in the past. She said *"this was good way for me to make some money."* I told her that I was not interested. I told her, *"I put my money on a "sure thing" which was God's business."* I told her that God would always give me more money back then I gave Him. I informed her that if she belonged to a church and she was not paying tithes at her church, she was *robbing God.* Well I didn't have to worry about her anymore with those foolish things. The word soon got around that I was one of those Christians. Good for Me! About three months later after the gambling situation, this same person came to me. She said, *"I need you to pray for me . . . I am about to lose my house. I haven't paid my house note in three months."* I was about to tell her to go to the casino and have those people pray for her. Go and tell them you are about to lose your house, see if they will help you. I promise you it was on the tip of my tongue! The only thing that stopped me was the *"Holy Spirit." Lord help me with my mouth!*

If you are not paying tithes and I knew your address, I would call the local police authorities. I would tell them to arrest you for committing a crime against the kingdom of God! You ask what crime have you committed and I say, *" you robbed God". You have committed a high crime that is subjected to high penalties or being miserable financially all of your life.* If you don't think you are robbing or cheating God read Malachi. The Word of God says in **Malachi 3:7-12 "Ever since the days of your ancestors, you have scorned my laws and failed to obey them. Now return to me, and I will return to you, says the Lord Almighty. But you ask, 'how can we return when we never gone away?' Should people cheat God? Yet you have cheated me! But you ask, what do you mean? When did we ever cheat you?' You have cheated me of the tithes and offerings due to me. You are under a curse, for your whole nation has been cheating me. Bring all the tithes into the storehouse so there will be enough food in my Temple. If you do, says the Lord Almighty, I will open the windows of heaven for you. I will pour out a blessing so great you won't have enough room to take it in! Try it! Let me prove it to you! " Your crops will be abundant, for I will guard them from insects and disease. Your grapes will not shrivel before they are ripe," says the Lord Almighty. Then all nations will call you blessed, for your land with be such a delight," says the Lord Almighty." I know that you probably read that Scripture fast, but did you read the part that says, " You are under a curse."* Let me be frank with you. I have enough trouble in my life, and I definitely don't want to be *"cursed"* by God. When you are cursed by God, the only one who can remove the curse is God! Do you remember in the Word of God when Saul consulted with a medium *(someone who preformed witchcraft).* He went to this medium to call up Samuel who was *dead.* Saul needed answers because God had pulled away from Saul. When the medium called up Samuel to give Saul advice, Samuel gave him a quick answer. The Word of God says in **I Samuel 28: 15-16**, he said, *"Why have you disturbed me by calling me back?" Samuel asked Saul. "Because I am in deep trouble," Saul replied. "The Philistines are at war with me, and <u>God has left me</u> and won't reply by prophets or dreams. So I have called for you to tell me what to do."* But Samuel replied, *"<u>Why ask me, since the LORD has left you and has become your enemy?</u>"* Did you see the part that says, *"God has left you."* Did you see the other part which says, *"the Lord has left you and has become your enemy."* **<u>As for me, I don't ever . . . . want to become an enemy of God!</u>** You can forget about going to see Sister Sara and all those folk who practice witchcraft. Those people have *no* power with Almighty God! So save your money! The Word of God is strong and real and He will do just what He said He will do. Do you think that God is bluffing and won't deliver, or do what He said He would do? For those of you that don't know God the way I know Him, God doesn't sell any *wolf tickets*. God has the power and the ability to back up everything He says.

People can make so many promises that they don't fulfill. Men will promise to bring you money on Tuesday to pay your utility bill before the disconnection on Wednesday. I would not trust him to give me the money to keep me and my children from being in the dark by Friday. When all is said and done, you will still be waiting on that man to come through for you. You will be looking for those candles when your power goes off, and trying to buy ice to keep your food from *"spoiling."* At the end of the day, you will still be in the dark, you will still be broke and God will still be **"The Provider."**

What is time and how is it measured? Time can be defined as a component of the measuring systems that can be used to sequence events, and also it can be used to compare the durations of events. We spent eight hours of our time on jobs in order to provide for ourselves or our families. Some folk work on jobs they hate, while others works on jobs they love. In both cases, both groups are spending eight hours or more of their time.

I know you've probably heard someone say, *"Don't waste my time, . . . or . . . you are wasting my time."* But let us stop and ask ourselves, are we *"wasting our own time?"* How much time have we spent on *"dead end relationships"* that go nowhere? And now the question becomes , *"how much <u>more</u> time should we give to this dead end relationship?"*

As children we learned how to count early by our parents. Our parents taught us how to count, first on one hand, and then the other hand. By the time we got to first grade, we could count to ten because we knew we had ten fingers. Later on in elementary school we graduated to counting by groups of five. We also jumped rope and counted by five's in order to remember our five time multiplication tables. That five time table have followed us all our adult lives, and we still remember, "*five, ten, fifteen . . . .*" But I say as adults, we should <u>put away</u> our five time tables and stop counting. The counting of five's have made some women remained in relationships way passed the time when they should have ended. Let me share my thoughts on "*five, ten, fifteen . . .*" in a relationship.

The trouble with some women is they waste too much time in relationships because they are in love. Being in love is a beautiful thing, and it can one day result in marriage, if you become a lady or remain a lady. Being "*lady like*" is just one of the factors <u>descent</u> men consider in choosing a wife. If you consider yourself marriage material the question becomes, "*how much time are you willing to wait to become his wife?*" I believe that if a young woman in her twenties has met a man, she <u>should not invest</u> over <u>five years</u> in that relationship without a proposal. Five years is enough time for her to get to know him and vice versa. Even though I am no authority on relationships, I believe that a woman should not spent over five years with any man without some type of ring. And please by no means, <u>" don't do a thing . . . if you don't have **both rings** on your finger."</u> I didn't say **"ring,"** I said **" rings",** meaning more than one! It shouldn't take him five years or more for him to decide whether or not you are worthy of being his wife.

Men always know what they want, and it doesn't take a man years to make a decision. A good of example of how long it takes a man to make a decision, check out his vehicle. <u>He can tell you the first time he saw that vehicle, and the day he fell in *love* with it!</u> Even though there were other vehicles around him, he noticed that <u>**one**</u> vehicle! Are you getting it? After falling in love with that <u>**one**</u> vehicle he *immediately* did his research. He found out the cost, the size of the motor and how fast the vehicle could run. He can also tell you the variety of colors of the vehicle and his color of choice. Now with all of that being said, "*don't you think that five years is enough time for him to do his research on* <u>**you**</u>?" He's already has an opinion of whether or not you are marriage material. Don't you his family members have given him their opinion of *whether* or *not* you are a "*good woman?*" Don't you think that he has noticed by now *whether* or *not* you are a good housekeeper or a good cook? I more than sure that he knows *whether* or *not* you can manage his money. He has made an observation of the way you manage your own money.

I made reference to a woman in her twenties, but this also goes for women in their thirties, forties, fifties and sixties. Women in their *fifties* and *sixties* should **not invest** that kind of time with Mr. Frank. She and Mr. Frank are closer to meeting "*their Maker*" then someone in their twenties. Sister girl don't have a lot of time to waste with Mr. Frank. Tell Mr. Frank, "after all this time, I am more than sure you have made your observations. I know that you have come to a conclusion . . . and if you cannot make decision . . . . I will make one for you." During this time Mr. Frank will probably *"catch a case of Alzheimer's"* and forgot he has been seeing you for the past five years or more! Don't be fooled, it's just a case of a *"failure to commit."* Tell him it's no more, "five, ten, fifteen" years from you. Tell him you got yourself together, and you finally woke up! Thank God for your decision, and stop counting by five's and start counting by one's!

MONEY, BODY AND TIME

I LOVE TO SPEND MONEY,
AND SHOP UNTIL I DROP.
SOME WOMEN MAKE THEIR MONEY,
BY SAYING, " A HUNDRED DOLLARS A WOP."

SHE IS WILLING TO SELL HER BODY,
FOR ALL THAT SHE CAN GET.
SHE'LL DO ANYTHING FOR MONEY,
AS LONG AS HER NEEDS ARE MET.

BUT DONT USE YOUR BODY,
TO GET WHAT YOU PLEASE,
FOR GOD IS STILL ABLE,
TO SUPPLY YOUR EVERY NEED.

by
Rita J. Rushing

Chapter 13

Is Prince Charming Still Charming?

As a child we all had our favorite storybook characters like The Three Little Pigs, Cinderella, and Snow White. The story of Cinderella and Snow White is a story that we all have read about or heard about. It's the story of two different, yet similar young women who encountered abuse and jealousy at the hands of two evil and wicked women. Both Cinderella and Snow White were both looking forward to being delivered or rescued from their dilemma. Finally, two men rescue them both. In these stories, both male characters are called, *"prince"*, and deemed as the one who rescued a damsel.

Today women are still waiting for their *"prince"* to come and rescue them. The women especially want to be rescued if they have been, or are in an abusive or neglecting relationship. Each time a woman is slapped, kicked, stomped, cussed out, or neglected in that relationship she wishes that a *"prince"* would come and rescue her. She is hurt, broken and in pain from all of the drama. Each day she hopes and prays that this *"frog"* who is abusive, would change into the *"prince"* from her childhood dreams. But if you will reflect back to your first encounter, you will be reminded that **you chose** that *"prince"* to be a part of your life. Cinderella was not to blame for her mistreatment; it was her mean stepmother, who Cinderella was forced live with who inflicted her pain. Snow White on the other hand, was given a poison apple that caused Snow White to fall into a deep sleep. It was the evil and jealous queen that wanted Snow White dead.

The question is, *"who is poisoning your mind and putting you into a deep "sleep" to make you think that he is a prince?"* The only way you're going to get your prince, you must seek the **"Prince of Peace"** and the **"Lord of lords."**

The Prince of Peace and Lord of lords know whether or not if *your prince* is authentic. He already knows whether he is faking on your behalf. Remember, women are not the only ones who *"put on airs."*. The *"prince"* that is send by the *"Prince of Peace and Lord of lords"* will come with a seal of approval and bear a *seal* of approval from the One who sent him. God already know that Women of God and Christians should *look for,* and receive an approval or confirmation from God as a sign of approval. But too often women of God or Christians don't ask God, or *want to know,* if God has sent that man.

I remember once when I was at a local drug store in the cosmetic area, a lady came to the counter to pay for a tube of mascara. She told us who were gathered at the counter, she was trying to *"spruce"* herself up. She said she had not put on makeup in two weeks since she put her husband out of *her* house. I told her that I was sorry to hear that her marriage had ended and she said, *"I'm not."* She went on to tell us that this man was a liar and no good. I asked her where did she meet this no good man, and she said, *"In the church."* She said he began attending her church and she already had ask God to send her a church going husband. She went on to describe his mannerism, clothing attire and how he studied the Bible. She said she just *knew* that God had sent him to her. Well, here I go with my inquisitive self! I said, *"well baby did you ask God if he was the man that He had sent and, did you ask God if you could marry that man?"* Suddenly she dropped her head and answered *"no"*. This woman had married this man, moved him into her house, only to find out that this man was legally married to another woman in another state.

There are two things wrong with this picture: *first* she didn't consult God her father and ask permission to marry this man and *secondly* she moved him in to *her . . . . house!* I have a problem with moving a man into my house. I just going to be honest about it, God knows that I have a problem with that issue. I cannot see *myself* allowing a man to come live in a house that God has provided for me. **What God has for me, it is for me!** You know the song! Now please don't get me wrong. I don't have a problem with us living together in my house until we purchase a house together, or until God blesses us with a house from the ground up. But to live permanently in my house that God has bless me with, I don't think so! That man is the head of the house. *As head of the house, it means that he better purchase a house for us, for him to be the head of . . . . and not mine!* I have heard about, and I know of some women personally, who have gotten put out of *"their own house"* by their new husbands. If a man thinks that he is going to put me *out of my own home,* he should be forewarned, he better bring some *"backup with him."* I will cut down everything that gets in my way! I said from the beginning, I still have issues that God is still working on with me!

Women for the most part will have more respect for a man, that has his own, and *can* carry his own wait. I have pulled enough excess baggage over the years. I've learned that all of the baggage that I carried was because I did *not consult* God in the first place! **Silly, silly me!** Don't be one of those women who would rather *chose* a man, or allow a *man to chose her,* the way the world chooses. The way the world chooses is with the eyes and ears. That **should not** be the way for us. We should consult God to hear what God says about that man! God is the only one who knows the motives and the outcome of all relationships, from the beginning to the end. Moreover, if we confess that God is our Father then go to God your Father.

Ask the Father first whether or *not* you can *spend time* with this man. This time spend includes going a movie, and all of the simple things we do on the norm. God already knows *"what that man"* is up to! God is an all seeing and all knowing God. After all, Father always knows best!

PRINCE CHARMING

I WANT TO BE A PRINCESS,
A PRINCESS IS ALWAYS SERVED,
OTHERS AROUND, SAY TO ME,
"GIRL YOU HAVE GOT SOME NERVE."

A PRINCESS ALWAYS NEEDS A PRINCE,
TO COME TO HER RESCUE.
BUT WHERE IS MY PRINCE CHARMING
THE ONE SO FAIR, SO TRUE?

MY PRINCE HAS FINALLY ARRIVED IN MY LIFE,
THE ONE I'VE DREAMED OF,
BUT NOW MY PRINCE IS NO LONGER CHARMING,
HE'S USING ME JUST BECAUSE.

HIS WAYS ARE NO LONGER CHARMING,
HE CHANGED ON ME YOU SEE.
FOR HE IS NO LONGER CHARMING,
BUT VERY MEAN TO ME.

I WAITED FOR HIM A LONG TIME,
IT SEEMS LIKE YEARS TO ME.
I HOPE THIS PRINCE WILL GO AWAY
SO GOD CAN RESTORE ME.

by
Rita J. Rushing

Chapter 14

BEING IN A RELATIONSHIP WITH AN
ABUSER OR LOSER OR BOTH

Being in an abusive relationship is like playing Russian roulette with only one bullet in the gun. Soon or later that one bullet will come out of that chamber, and bang, your dead. I cannot understand for the love of me how some women can allow someone to beat, slap or belittle them at anytime. I guess the reason why I cannot understand is because I have always *loved myself* more than <u>any</u> man! Well you may say that is being selfish, and perhaps your right. But I can tell you this! I never had a busted lip, broken bones, a black eye or any other scars associated with a beating! No one has ever choked me, nor have I had any blood drawn from me that was inflicted by the hands of another human being. Heaven help him if he did!

Whenever I would enter a relationship with a man I would make sure that I would bring up the subject of violent men. I would then listen and observe his response during that conversation. I would make sure that I would look into his eyes and check his body language when he gave me his answer. I never got so *"caught up"* just being with him not to listen and observe his responses. When someone is lying they will sometimes look down or shift their eyes to draw your attention away from the answer. Some men go so far as to reach out and grab your hand or stroke your face. This is nothing but a *"ploy"* to assure you that he would never hurt you. He knows you want him and he must convince you to trust and believe in him in the first place. You know it's been awhile since someone has held your hand or stroked your face ever so gently. He deliberately touches you to make you lose all perspectives. It is a trick of the enemy!

It is very important for women to make a stand against violent behavior. During my conversation with a man, I make it perfectly clear that I will *not enter* or *remain* in a relationship with a man who was abusive. Not only that, I made sure that he knows that I am not alone. I tell him about my " *two little friends"* called Smith and Weston who I keep around as an added bonus for my safety. The respond that I usually receive after making that statement was, *"that's a mighty big gun."* Men are usually familiar with types of firearms and I want them to know they are not the only one who knew about firearms. I also emphasize my marksmanship in hitting my target as well. Keep in mind, during this time I was not a born again Christian! But thanks be to God, I am a born again Christian.

If I was not a born again Christian, I probably would have *shot* those furniture mover who held my furniture hostage. God has taught me, how to *control me!* I am a work in progress, because I still have issues. God is still teaching me to give situations to Him and not take the matter into my own hands. I have cried *"real tears"* and *"begged"* God to let me say something or do something to someone who has made me *"mad."* But He said **"No"** I have tried to *bargain* with God by saying, *"if you just let me say one thing . . . "* God said, **"No."** I have cried in the presence of other people who have *"ticked"* me off. Then they look at me and say, *"why are you crying?"* I tell them, *"I am crying because God will <u>not allow me</u> to say what I want to say, or do what I want to do to you!."* I hope that I will always be *obedient* to God and not allow my lack of self control to become *disobedient* to God. As far as my weapon is concerned, God has *not told me* to give up my Smith and Weston. And if God is not *"saying nothing, I ain't doing nothing."*

As I stated earlier, I cannot understand what would make a woman, especially a Christian woman take abuse from an individual. The Word of God says in **John 3:16 . . .**"*that God so loved the world the world that He gave His only begotten Son, that whosoever believeth on Him should not perish but have everlasting life."* If God so loved the world and you are living <u>in this world</u>, why would you allow someone to try and take you out of the same world that He sent His Son to save? Jesus said in **Matthew 10:39,** *" He that findeth his life shall lose it: and he that loseth his life for my sake shall find it."* Jesus is not asking you to *lose* your life for His sake. This person is trying to take your life for <u>his sake.</u> It's the control, dominance, and abuse that are the true factor, not Jesus calling you to come home to be with Him!

One of the sad thing about the death of someone who died from being abused, the person who committed the crime, has *no resurrection* power. He *cannot* or *will not* resurrect you by no means! When you leave planet Earth, there is no returning! You may have been made *by him,* to believe that he was "*Lord and Savior.*" **Make no mistake, He is not the Lord!** When that man stands over your coffin telling you he is sorry, it will not bring you back. The tears that he will cry, if he cries at all, will not bring you back. There is only one person that ever walked on planet Earth that can restore or giving you eternal life after death and his name is J-E-S-U-S.

Some women do survive the abuse, while others do not. If you are one of those who are blessed to be alive, be mindful that as you get older those broken bones don't heal as quickly as they once did. Those teeth that you brushed twice a day, and used whitening toothpaste to keep white, can be replaced when he knocks them out. But good teeth don't come cheap. I know where you can get a mouthful of dentures or porcelain veneers. Folk now a day are getting porcelain veneers which are expensive! The teeth are beautiful, yet costly. You are better off keeping your own teeth and keeping every bone in your body in place and get out of the relationship.

I know that some women keep the secret of being abused. They are afraid to tell someone, afraid that someone would suggest to leave that situation. But this is one secret that you need to tell. You should broadcast to anyone who will listen and <u>help you get out.</u> Don't worry about the time and money you say you have *invested* in the relationship. You are about to make a far greater investment than the one you are leaving. *You are investing in your life, your sanity and peace of mind.*

Much too often people put a material value on their life by counting their personal possessions. They are quick to say, "*Oh he pays all of my bills, or he helps me pay some of my bills*". But guess what? **He is also helping to kill you why he is making contributions to your wallet!** The question becomes, "*are you willing to give up your life for money or worldly possessions?*" Once you decide to leave that abusive situation, don't allow him to put you a *"guilt trip."* He will probably say, "*you want to put me out now that I have paid for your car. I helped you catch up on all your bills and took care of you and your children. I know you have a little money saved and it's all because you saved your money and spent mine . . . now you want to put me out . . . you used me . . . . and now . . . you don't want me no mo.!*" You tell him I said, *"fair exchange, no robbery"!* He also reaped the benefits of living in *sin* with you as well. As far as I am concerned it was a *"fair exchange, and no robbery was committed".*

Both of you are guilty of committing a sin. *What is honor among thieves and what is sin among sinners?* I believe that when a woman gives her body to a man she has nothing else to give. She has given him a temple that should be held <u>exclusively</u> for God, until God releases her to be with the mate He has chosen for her.

The only person that who maybe benefiting from this abuse, is the person who is doing the abusing. Because he is abusing you, he no longer has to go to the gym or exercise to stay in shape. All the slapping and punching that you receive will keep his muscles strong and keep him buffed up. The stomping and dragging he does, like you are a *"side of beef"*, will keep his calves in his legs strong and muscular. If you think there is no end to this torment and you have no way out, you are wrong. There is a way out and someone is waiting to protect from the hands of the enemy. God is waiting with His arms stretched wide ready and able to receive you. God is able to keep you safe from harm and danger, and He assures us in His written word. If you don't know where to look in the Bible, read **Psalms 91.** The Word of God says in **Psalm 91:4**, *"He shall cover thee with his feathers and under his wings shalt thou trust: his truth shall be thy shield and buckler."* There is no better protection then the protection that God provides! **Psalm 91:11-12** also says, *" <u>For he shall give his angels charge over thee, to keep thee in all thy ways. They shall bear thee up in their hands, lest thou dash thy foot against a stone.</u> "* Psalm 91 is one of my favorite chapters in the Bible.

I am reminded of the first time I saw *one* of my guardian angels. I only said one because I know that we have several, whose job is to watch over us. I remember one day I was getting dressed for work when I saw one of my angels. I had just finished praying on my knees and got up to put on my sandals. While I was strapping my left sandal, I looked to my left side and I saw a huge being standing next to me with his arms fold like Mr. Clean, the character on the cleaning solution. I could not see his face because he appeared to be over ten feet tall. I remember one of his legs and thighs appeared to be bigger than my whole body, at least twice the size of a telephone pole. When I saw him I was not afraid, because I had just finished praying and I knew that I was still in the *"spirit"*. I continued to strap my sandal and I began to speak to him. I said, *"oh I see you . . . I know who you are . . . you are my angel."* He stood right there and did not move or speak. When I finished strapping my sandal and got up and put both feet on the floor and start moving. He immediately began moving right next to me. I began thanking and praising God for his protection and cried while I continued to get dressed. Even to this day as I write about this occurrence it brings tears to my eyes. What a wonderful feeling and assurance to know that God is watching me and provided me with

His protection. This is the main reason we can be <u>assured</u> that God will provide the protection that abused women need in order to get out of situations. I want you to know that I am *not* the only person that God protects. He will protect you too! *God is no respecter of persons!* God does *not love* me anymore than He *loves you;* and if He is protecting me he can also protect you as well.

AN ABUSER AND A LOSER

YOU GOT NERVE TO BEAT ME?
I PLAITED YOUR HAIR AND WASHED YOUR CLOTHES YOU SEE,
EVEN PREPARED YOUR BATH AND BATHED YOU LIKE A BABY.
AND YOU COME IN THIS HOUSE AND BEAT ME LIKE YOU
CRAZY!

TELL ME, WHAT I DID WRONG?
FOR EACH DAY YOU CAME FROM WORK INTO A CLEAN HOME,
FLO' SO CLEAN, YOU CAN SUCK MILK WITH A STRAW.
I'M TALKIN' BOUT SQUEAKY CLEAN,
AND YOU COME IN ACTING SO MEAN.

THEN YOU LEAVE, STAY OUT ALL NIGHT LONG.
GONE SO LONG, I THOUGHT I WAS LIVING ALONE.

MY MOMMY TOLD ME TO LEAVE, BUT I WOULDN'T TAKE HEED,
MAN YOU REALLY CAUSE MY PO' HEART TO BLEED.

ONE DAY I LOOKED IN THE MIRROR, WHAT I SAW SCARED ME,
I LOOKED LIKE A RACOON AND SAID "HOW CAN THIS BE?"

MY FRIENDS SAY, "GUL, YOU LET THAT MAN BEAT YOU LIKE A
FOOL,
YET YOU TREAT HIM LIKE A KING."
I SAY,"I THOUGHT I KNEW LOVE, IF YOU KNOW WHAT I MEAN "

ONE DAY I CALLED UP ON THE LORD AND ASKED HIM TO HELP
ME,
I SAY GOD FROM THIS MAN PLEASE SET ME FREE!

by
Cynthia J. Simmons

Chapter 15

TAKING WOODEN NICKELS AND MAKING CHANGE

As a child I can remember adults telling other adults not to take any *"wooden nickels."* I was very naïve with worldly things as a child and I thought there was such a thing as an actual *"wooden nickel."* I never saw the *"wooden nickel"*, but I knew it existed because the adults would tell others not to take any *"wooden nickels."* After years of trying to find a *"wooden nickel"* I finally found out as a young adult the meaning of not taking a *"wooden nickel."* I grew up in a era when children asked adults questions you would never get a straight answer, or they would say, *"go sit down and stay out grown folks conversations"*. When I became a young lady someone took the time to explain to me the meaning of not taking any *"wooden nickels."* I was told the meaning meant, *" not let anyone tell me a lie or bunch of lies and believe it."* It also meant, *" not to let anyone make a fool out of me, and that I should be wise in dealing with other people in general"*. I thought about the **"wooden nickels"** and what it meant for quite some time. I knew that I **never** wanted anyone to try and give me a *"wooden nickel!"*

I remember special prayers growing up as a young lady. While others my age was praying for bicycles or a new pair of rollers skates, I would be praying for wisdom. As a child I saw so much *"silliness"* I knew that I would need help from God not be *"silly"* or *"foolish."* Mama always made sure we knew how to pray, especially, **The Lord's Prayer!** You know how to say the Lord's Prayer right? At the end of the prayer, I would pray my *"silly* and *"foolish"* prayer as well. I would say something like, *"Lord I saw Joyce get beat down today like a "dog" . . . I saw her being punched, slapped and* *drugged down the street . . . help me oh Lord to never be "silly" like Joyce . . . . and heaven help the man if he does . . . Amen."*

I saw so many silly and foolish women running behind no good men. I saw these women taking care of men, allowing men to beat them and cheat on them. I told God that I was <u>not wise enough</u> to know a man's heart, but I wanted God to keep the **"no good men"** and **"dirty men"** away from me. I asked God to give me the wisdom to know the difference between the" *good men"* and the *"no good men."* I thank God that He did just what I asked of Him. Whenever I would meet a man that was interested in me, my liar radar would go up. I was in position ready to receive any incoming lies that was coming my way. Don't get me wrong. I have encountered some *"no good men."* I believe that God was allowing me to meet such men, in order for *me to know* if I could recognize the difference in men. How will you know if you have received what you asked for? When the lies start coming in, then I would begin my *questioning!* My mother use to say to me when I was a little girl, **"Rita, you ask too many question, or you are too noisy."** Little did she and I know, my inquisitive mind would take me much further in life than she or I could ever imagine! One thing is for sure, my mother knew people would not make a fool out of me. Nor would I take any *"wooden nickels!"*

I never knew what other women would go through in a relationship until I became a grown woman and moved out on my own. As I formed adult relationships with other women, I realized that some of these women were so *silly* and had not matured to the degree for their age group. I soon found out that many of them were taking care of men. I found out that some women were giving men, some, if not all, of their hard earned money. Back in the day, women worked much harder than women today. Most of the jobs held by women during those times was domestic work. There is no way I am going to mop someone's floors or clean their toilets and give a man one dime of my money. Where was he when I was cleaning that filthy toilet? Now he's looking up in my face for a *"hand out"*. Women back then would bail men out of jail when needed. Not only would a woman bail a man out of jail, but she would bail him out of jail, <u>even if he went to jail for beating her!</u> *I wish I catch myself bailing a man out of jail who went to jail for beating me in the first place!* I want you to take me to an open field and beat me like a **"Hebrew slave."** And by no means, have **no** mercy on me! If I am that stupid, I don't need mercy!

I also found out that women would allow their husbands or boyfriends to see other women. These women would know about these other women and when the man didn't show up, they would go to the other woman's house and leave a message. Often times the two women would fight like *"cats and dogs"* in the middle of the street. The man would stand by and watch these two street fighters go at each other. In the end he would leave with the woman he *"benefitted"* from the most. Married men would stay away from their families for days and show up later like nothing happened. He would come home like he had been sleeping with his wife all that time. You would hear some cussing for a while, but it soon died down and later you smelled food being cooked for her *"in and out"* husband. She continues to take those *"wooden nickels!"* This is so disrespectful. No respect for his wife, his children or his home! It couldn't be me.

These women would do anything to keep those men in their lives, including having babies out of wedlock. Her plan is to trap him into marrying her, or stay in the relationship with her. But to their dismay, it didn't work and the men still did not commit to marriage. The men continue to cheat while she was pregnant and after the birth of the child. To bring a child into the world can be a wonderful thing if both parents are married to each other. But to have a baby out of wedlock to trap a man is stupid, especially when you know he is a liar, cheater and he is broke! Now that the baby is there, it comes with added responsibilities and expenses. Today women are still having babies out of wedlock and at their own expense and at times, at the expense of the taxpayers. If you **cannot** afford to provide food, clothing and shelter for your baby without the federal government's assistance, then stop having children! Just close your legs! He is not going to marry you anyway. You can't keep your legs closed long enough! It is rare that a man will marry a woman with two, three or more children. He wants to start his own family, and the majority of the time, his family will advise him not marry a woman with that many children.

Starting a family is a decision that will impact you for the rest of your life. When your parents gave birth to you they expect you to grow up, get a good job, become a productive citizen, and marry someone that would be good to you. They also expected you to move out of the home, go to college and someday have your *own* home with your *own* husband. The last thing on the mind of your parents would be their young daughter would grow up and be *silly*. Mother had no idea that you would allow a man to come and live with you without the benefit of marriage, because after all, she didn't raise you that way. She could never imagine that you would be the one going to work, while he stayed at your house and not work. *Here we go again, your . . . . house!* No one could convince your father that his little girl would allow a man to drop her off at work and drive her car up and down the streets, using her gas while he searches for women. Oh yes, he drives your car and you know. He even goes so far as to say it belongs to him. This is the reason why your friends come back and tell you they saw another woman in your vehicle. Keep in mind every woman does not work, and some women work nights. He has plenty of time to ride and shine in your truck or car. I wish I catch myself allowing a man to take my truck and drop me off at work each and every day. Long ago when someone ask how were we going to get to place we would say by *"TP&W."* That means," Take the Pain and Walk." So the next time he ask to use your . . . . vehicle, tell him to use his own transportation which is TP&W the most reliable transportation in the country.

As women of God we must remember, *"What God has for me, it is for me."* That means you should not allow someone to come into your life and *destroy* everything that God has given you. Let him go out and acquire his own possessions and allow God to bless *him* with his own. There is nothing wrong with telling someone *"no"* and you *don't* have to feel guilty about saying *"no"*. Some people can't say *"no,"* or are not willing to say "no", and because you cannot say *"no"* you will never have anything. If you cannot say *"no"* then just say *"nay."* Even in the Bible the answer was either, *"yea"* or *"nay."* And if the person don't know what "yea" or *"nay"* means, tell them to look it up and don't *you* give in to their demands!

Some of you make think that you have made too many mistakes with him. You feel you may as well continue on the same path in hopes of him changing. *Don't wait on him to change, you change!* You should change the way you relate to men, come out of that horror, and return to the God of Abraham, Isaac and Jacob. He is the same God that brought the Israelites out of Egypt, and the same God that changed the mind of Pharaoh. He is the same God that can change anything. **The Word of God** says in **Proverbs 1:1** ***"The Lord can control a king's mind as he controls a river; he can direct it as he pleases."*** You don't have the power to change the mind or the heart of that man, only God can fulfill that task. You must stop taking *"wooden nickels"* and *"stop waiting for a change"* to occur. The greatest change that will occur in anyone's life is when they ask Jesus Christ to come in their life, and totally surrender to him. <u>As long as that man thinks you love him more than you love God, no change will occur.</u> As long as he believes that <u>you love him</u> more than <u>yourself</u>, he will always give you *"wooden nickels"* and *you* will always be waiting for change!

YOU REMIND ME OF ME

YOUR QUALITIES ARE SUCH
OF GRACE, LOVE AND HONESTY.
I SEE APART OF MYSELF;
YOU REMIND ME OF ME.

GOD GAVE YOU WISDOM,
FROM THE TIME OF YOUR BIRTH,
THAT YOU CAN MAKE WISE DECISIONS,
HERE ON PLANET EARTH.

YOU WERE TAUGHT NOT TO FALL,
FOR GAMES FROM ANY MAN,
AND ACCEPT *"WOODEN NICKELS"* OUT OF NO MAN'S HANDS!

by
C. J. Simmons

Chapter 16

WISDOM IS THE KEY

There are some Christian women who are involved, become involved or remain in relationships because of sexual fulfillment, lack of finances, loneliness or for the sake of the children. Even though women are aware that Jesus Christ is not in the relationship, they are willing to form or remain linked up with these men. But I say to you, "*don't allow yourself to get caught up in conversations and form relationships with non-Christians in order to fill that void in your life*". A man once told me, "*never give a man too much conversation, because it will give him something to go on.*" I didn't understand what it meant at the time, but I know now! The more women talk to men, the more the men think they are getting someplace with you. The length of time you spend "*conversing*" with that man is a clear indicator of your interest in him as well.

There are women who have told me that they have male friends who they talk to for hours over the telephone. When I question the purpose of this friendship, someone would say, "*well I talk to him just to hear a male voice or we talk about the Lord*". My question is, "*what do you talk about after you stop talking about "The Lord"*"? Nobody talks about "*The Lord*" twenty-four hours a day, not even the Pope! When does the conversation change from "*The Lord*" and turn to your personal likes and dislikes? The next thing you know the two of you will arrange some sort of meeting to "*talk as friends.*" I hope that when the two of you meet you will you take the "*Holy Spirit*" with you on this encounter and every encounter afterwards. You are going to need the "*Holy Spirit*" to discern any lies that may come your way. Be cautious and don't get too excited in that you don't use your ears to listen.

As women of God if you can't take the *"Holy Spirit"* with you, then you probably don't need to go yourself. If you don't have the *"Holy Spirit"* in your conversation maybe you should <u>hang up the telephone</u> and stop the conversations all together. Some women **don't** and **won't** bring up the conversation of God in their lives. They are not willing to express their relationship with God in fearing of losing that man's interest. As for me, I let a man know *"straight off the bat"* my relationship with God. A man once said to me, **"Rita, you talk about God more than some ministers I know. You talk about God so much it might run a man off."** I said to him, **"honey, I want that man to know my position with God. I want to make sure that man knows that I am a child of the Most High God and I love God and I am not ashamed."** I went on to say, **"when I talk about God to that man it will do one or two things; that man will either run to me, or run away from me, and either way God will be glorified."** The next thing he said to me was, *"see it don't bother me at all."* God still gets the glory. This is what I mean when I say that a *"man will either run to you or run from you!"*

The more personal the conversations become, the more intimate it will eventually become. The next thing you know you are in a sexual relationship with this man. This relationship is not of God and is not pleasing to God. After you have become involved with this man you realize that you have *"bitten off more"* than you can chew. You then try to rationalize your decision for becoming involved with him in the first place. Now you are in a defensive mode, and you try to defend your decision. You start saying stupid stuff like, *"oh I didn't know that he was like that,* "or *"girl he changed on me, I thought he was saved."* Now you are crushed when you realize he wasn't all you thought he was *"cracked up to be."*

Some women will go so far as to suggest the man played games, deceived or tricked them to win them over. It's not that he tricked you my dear, ... he *made a fool out of you!* The only reason a woman would make such excuses is to *try* and convince someone that it was the man fault. She does not want to appear as a foolish woman or be called a *"silly woman."* Not only that, she does not want anyone to know that she is *"silly"* and not as *perceptive* as she appears to others. The bottom line is Satan was setting her up because he knows how desperate she is to have a man in her life. It is better that you confess to yourself that he made a fool out of you, so you can heal and go on with your life.

Admit your faults and blame <u>no one</u> for your lack of discerning good character in that man. We all have faults and sometimes lack good judgment in determining the character of another person. This is why it is important that we allow the *"Holy Spirit"* to discern for us and determine what is best for our lives. I believe that the devices of men <u>do not</u> and <u>cannot</u> deceive women of God who read The Word of God and who is led by the *"Holy Spirit!"*

The fact of the matter is, Christian women *choose* to ignore all the warning signs that the *"Holy Spirit"* gives concerning these men. When women of God ignore the warnings and prompting of the *"Holy Spirit"*, and their relationship falls apart, then they want *sympathy* from others. *There are people who don't want to hear those sad stories because you knew that man was not a Christian from day one!* You took it upon yourself to become an *"overnight evangelist"* to convert this man to your liking. Perhaps you used poor judgment altogether. I say don't despair there is hope and a *cure* for your bad decisions, and it's called *wisdom.*

Wisdom, who said you lack wisdom? I say you lack wisdom, and it is evident in the choices you have made in the past. Wisdom is the key to making the right choices in all of life decisions. The Word of God tells us in **Proverbs 4:7,** *"Wisdom is the principal thing; therefore get wisdom: and with all thy getting get understanding."* Believe it or not it is very important to pray each day to God to bless <u>us</u> with spiritual wisdom, spiritual understanding and spiritual knowledge. It is necessary to pray in these areas in order to *discern* who and what is of God. Wisdom, understanding and knowledge will reveal to you any lies or any means of deception that is trying to enter, or remain in your life. *Without the wisdom of God you will be operating on your own discernment, and we all know what that has brought in your life.* So I say, arm yourself with the wisdom of God and pray that God will make you as wise as Solomon!

WOMAN OF WISDOM

GIRL! LET ME ASK YOU:
WHAT IS WRONG WITH YOU?
WHY ARE YOU ACCEPTING ALL THAT ABUSE?

HE COMES IN AND TELLS YOU BITTER LIES
CAN YOU NOT SEE THAT'S SATAN IN DISGUISE?

GO ON, OPEN UP YOUR SPRIUTAL EYES.
WALK LIKE GOD CREATED YOU, A WOMAN WHO IS WISE!

by
Cynthia J. Simmons

Chapter 17

WAITING OF THE PROMISES OF GOD

Just like many of you who are now reading this book, I too have not always been a Christian and *"silly."* I was baptized as a child and become a born again Christian in 1998. When I became born again, I *totally surrender my life and my body to God.* I lost friends after I surrendered to God. I no longer had the desire to go places I use to go, or do the things I use to do. I made a choice to do what was pleasing to God. I could *care less* what no one else thought about my decision, that included my family and my friends.

The most difficult thing I had to deal with surrendering my life to God was being alone and being lonely. I would dread weekends because this was the time that the devil would remind me of the fact that I was alone. Heretofore, before I became a born again Christian, I would always make sure that I was entertaining or being entertained. I can remember a comment that was made to me during the time that I was surrendering my life to God. His comment made me realize that the journey on the road to Jesus Christ would be long and difficult. He and I had a platonic relationship and we would often go to movies or out to dinner. We would do *just" plain stuff."* He would visit my home and sometimes I would cook dinner and we would just talk. I later found out that he was interested in me in another way and he wanted to be intimate and have a relationship. I explained to him from the beginning that I was trying get closer to God and find out who I was and whose I was. Once he expressed his interest in being intimate with me, I told him I wasn't about to do that. I told him that we could continue to be friends and we could go Dutch whenever we went out. Whenever he and I would go places I would offer to pay for my own meals or buy my own tickets, but it was he who insisted that he pay for everything. When I said that we could continue to come to go out and watch movies he said to me, *"Rita, I can watch a movie at my own house!"* I said, *"okay that's fine, you stay at your house and I will stay at mine!"* When I hung up the telephone with him I was hurt, and I cried. I did *not* cry because I was in love with him, but I cried because he was the only single male friend who I could go places with at that time. I didn't have to worry about him wanting something else from me, so I thought. After I hung up I called out to my God and I said, *"God is this the way it will be with me and men?"* God said, *"yes".* I then said to God with tearing screaming down my face, *"God so let it be done, so let it be written!"* I know this may sound crazy but I am so glad that happened. At that point and time, I made the decision to be alone and not compromise to please <u>my flesh</u>, or in this case, <u>his flesh!</u>

As women of God we should never compromise and engage in things of the world no matter how great the pressure, and no matter what we have to give up in order to please God. Saying yes to God, meanings saying no to the world. The world is full of people who are willing to forget about morals, values and abandon their relationship with God. For those who are willing to please self, or to please others, I say go for it.

If you are willing to be competitive to gain attention from someone, trust me, you will have to compete for the remainder of the relationship. You will find yourself constantly defending and comparing yourself to others. Let's not forget about the man's role of him constantly reminding you of <u>what</u> and <u>whom</u> he gave up for you.

Instead of studying women of the world or possibly your competition, study women of the Bible who held their <u>own weight and in their own right.</u> Read and study the women of the Bible who can be inspirational while you wait on God to bless you.

One of my favorite women in the Bible is **Ruth**. Ruth did not ask God for a husband, but God knew exactly what she needed. Not only did God send her a husband, He sent her the richest man in the county. Oh what a blessed woman! One day I was in my yard, my young neighbor, who is in twenties, came over to talk to me while I was washing my truck. He said that I needed a husband or a man. He said, *"Ms. Rita, you know, all you do is go to work and go to church, Ms Rita you need a husband. You don't have a man or nothing. I know that you get lonely sometimes . . . and need somebody to hold, cause everybody needs somebody to hold. I know you need somebody to hold Ms. Rita, because you are no different from nobody else, and everybody needs somebody."* I told him that I was waiting on God to send me own husband.

I explained to him that I was *not about to go* and look for a man. I told him that when God gets ready, God would arrange the meeting place and the time of meeting for my husband and me. When I went inside I began to think about what he said and his observation of me. One of the things he said was, *"all I did was go to work and to church."* This young had observed that I didn't have a man or men coming in or out of my house, or staying overnight at my house. This young man didn't realize what he said to me. To some it may have been a complaint! In actuality he was giving me compliments, and he didn't even know it. God knew that Satan had just used this young man to try and make me feel lonely. Satan wanted me to feel foolish for waiting on God, so I went inside my home and talked to God immediately. God said to me, *"I, (God) will not be mocked and you will not be put to shame for following Me."* I felt in my spirit that God was telling me, *"yes they may be laughing or talking about you now, because you trust Me; but I, (God) will do what I say I am going to do."* The very next day went I went to Sunday church service. One of the Scriptures that my congregation read in church was **Psalm 25,** in which David talks to God.

David said in **Psalm 25, 1-3,** *" Unto you O Lord, do I bring my life. O my God, I trust, lean on, rely on, and am confident in You. Let me not be put to shame or be disappointed; let not my enemies triumph over me. Yes, let none who trust and wait hopefully and look for You be put to shame or be disappointed; let them be ashamed who forsake the right or deal treacherously without cause."* While I was reading the scripture with the rest of the congregation tears rolled down my face and I wept. God brought back to me the conversation that I had with my young neighbor the day before. I knew that God was giving me confirmation from *His Holy Word* telling me to wait on Him and that I would not be disappointed for waiting on Him. God will fulfill his promise to you, and to me. Those same people who may have laughed or mocked you and I will have to come back someday and eat their own words.

Yes being alone and being lonely can be difficult, but what do you do? *I can tell you what I don't do, and that is having men coming to my house just to keep from being alone.* I don't engage in conversations with men over the telephone just to remind me that I am still a woman, desirable and still *"got it together."* As long as I have **God the Father**, **God the Son** and **God the Holy Spirit** in my life, I know that *"I have it together!"* God already assured me of that when He said, *"I belong to Him."* I don't lead men to think that something could someday come out of a relationship, whether it's a telephone conversation or face to face visits.

I have made up in my mind to wait on God no matter what it feels like or looks like. I just don't say one thing to sound good and do something else. Turning away from the things of the world and the ways of the world takes discipline. I have called my body to be in subjection for God. I have been celibate for over <u>ten years</u> and that just fine with me!

My friends asked "how did I do that?" I tell them I prayed and ask God to let my *"womanly"* feelings lie in a resting state until my husband stir them up on my wedding night. One of my friends said *she was not* going to ask God to do that, because she was not ready to give up sex. What she fail to realize its' not about sex. It's about being *obedient* to God! I was doing what the Word of God says to do concerning sex. **1 Corinthians 7:9** *"But if they can't control themselves, they should go ahead and marry. It's better to marry than to burn with lust."* <u>I don't care who is doing what, it is not for ME.! I promised God a long time ago that I would not sleep with another man until HE sends me my husband.</u> I want my husband to wake up anything in me that has been *"sleeping"* on my wedding night, and not before that time. I had women to ask me if I miss having sex. I tell them *"yes"*, but I don't miss it enough to compromise my walk with God. It takes discipline.

Being disciplined will cause you to give up a lot of things, but the rewards are much greater than what you gave up to follow Christ. Always be mindful of what is going on around you; and the types of people you're dealing with. There are forces much greater than you can imagine that we are dealing with, which are Satan and his people. Don't ever think that you can persuade or convert someone to Christ. It is highly unlikely the person will follow you and Jesus Christ. This conversion must be something the person's wants in his or her life. Leave the evangelism to someone who is called by God to convert that man and stop trying to rehabilitate him on your own. You just walk in your gift!

Use the time that God has allowed to work on your strength and weakness for the task ahead, because after all, our role is to make disciples for Christ. When you allow yourself to get caught up in drama that is time you could have spent serving God, or developing a closer relationship with God.

Whenever we are consumed with our own *drama* and the *drama* of other people it puts that *drama* on the front burner and God on the back burner! Everyone knows that whatever is on the front burner will be watched or taken care of more than the back burner; and if we are not careful, what is on the back burner will burn up.

Over the years in my walk with God I have learned so much, and I still have much more to learn. My learning process will not be complete until God calls me home to be with him. The things I have learned I have shared with you. I hope that *"Silly Women"* has been an enlightenment to you and cause you to self examine your personal life.

I have learned that God always provides. If I tell you how many times and the miracles God has performed in my life, some of you would not believe it. God's provision is always more than enough and God *will not* and *cannot* lie. The Word of God says in **Numbers 23:19,** " *God is not a man, that he should lie, nor a son of man, that he should change his mind. Does he speak and then not act? does he promise and not fulfill?*" Always remember God cannot lie to you or me. His promises are solid as "**The Rock.**"

I am no different from many of you who are waiting on God. I know that God does not need my help in the selection of my mate, and I know He knows what is best for me. I trust God more than I trust myself or any other human being, and I don't believe everything everyone says. God has shown me over the years who will fail and who will not fail. Please note, God never failed me. I don't believe what men say to me, only what God says to me. I have caught so many lies, and the only excuse they gave was, "*I changed my mind*". I "*changed my mind*" might work for you, but it doesn't cut it with me.

I have been writing this book for many years, as a matter of fact it has taken me seven years. The "*Holy Spirit*" would wake me up every night at different times and talk to me. He would wake me up from a "*deep sleep*" and just start talking to me. I was told to write this information down. I had no clue as to why I was writing this down, or what I was going to do with the information. After I had about three to five legal size tablets of this information I questioned God and asked what should I do with this information. God spoke to me and said, "*You're going to write a book.*" I said, "*Lord what will I call it.?*" The Lord spoke to me and said, "*Silly Women.*" I repeated it several times back to God. I said, "*Lord I don't want to call anyone silly, he said, "Silly Women.*" When I was given this title, I went on the Internet and typed the word, "*silly women.*" Tears filled my eyes! *Silly Women* was in the Bible. It was not me calling women "*Silly*" the **Word of God** calls them "*Silly.*"

It says in **II Timothy 3: 1-7,** "*This know also, that in the last days perilous times shall come. ²For men shall be lovers of their own selves, covetous, boasters, proud, blasphemers, disobedient to parents, unthankful, unholy, ³Without natural affection, trucebreakers, false accusers, incontinent, fierce, despisers of those that are good, ⁴Traitors, heady, highminded, lovers of pleasures more than lovers of God; ⁵Having a form of godliness, but denying the power thereof: from such turn away. ⁶For of this sort are they which creep into houses, and lead captive silly women laden with sins, led away with divers lusts, ⁷Ever learning, and never able to come to the knowledge of the truth.*

Here is another version of **II Timothy 3:1-7,** ""*You should also know this that in the last days there will be very difficult times. For people will love only themselves and their money. They will be boastful and proud, scoffing at*

God, disobedient to their parents and ungrateful. They will consider nothing sacred. They will be unloving and unforgiving, they will slander others and have no self-control; they will be cruel and have no interest in what is good. They will betray their friends, be reckless, be puffed up with pride and love pleasure rather than God. They act as if they are religious, but they will reject the power that could make them godly. You must stay away from people like that. They are the kind who work their way into people's homes and win the confidence of <u>vulnerable women</u> who are burdened with the guilt of sin and controlled by many desires. Such women are forever following new teachings, but they never understand the truth."

Over the years I have received numerous confirmations from God to go forth and write this book. One confirmation I received was in my kitchen. I was washing dishes, listening to the radio and thinking about women and the things women do in the church. The man of God on the radio said something in his sermon about the very same thing I was thinking about at that time. I almost dropped the plate I was washing in the sink, and I could not wash another dish. I had to sit and compose myself. I immediately spoke to God about what the man of God said on the radio. I said, *"God should I say that in my book"* God spoke to me and said. *"Say it."* I knew then without a shadow of a doubt I was to suppose to continue to write this book and include in my book the very thing I thought about and he spoke about.

When I started writing this book the *"Holy Spirit"* told me what to write about in this book. I know some of the things that I wrote about were vulgar or too brash for some, but I was guided by the *"Holy Spirit."* **God told me to say it, and I am going to say it! It does not matter what people think of me or say about me. I have no allegiance with man, my only allegiance is with God!** The *"Holy Spirit"* has already revealed that some folk will frown at me and talk behind my back. I know that I will lose some friends. These things matter less to me. The only thing important to me, is being obedient to God! The Word of God says, *"obedience is better than sacrifice."* I have chosen to sacrifice <u>my friends</u> and be obedient to <u>My God</u>!

People are always looking for fulfillment, especially women. Women look for something to satisfy, rather than the true Word of God to free them. Men are able to recognize the need for satisfaction and they will prey upon weak-willed women. Don't allow deception to enter and remain in your life. Pray for wisdom and learn your mistakes, as I have learned and will continue to learn from mine. Free yourself from worldly pleasures, desires or passions and stand firm for God. The world may be going to *"hell in a hand basket"* but we don't have to follow the world and go to hell with them. While the world is going astray, we should be about our Father's business, which is making disciples for Christ. The Word of God says in **Matthew 28:19, 20,** *"Go therefore and make disciples of all nations, baptizing them in the name of the Father, and the Son and of the Holy Spirit, and teaching them to obey everything that I have commanded you. And remember, I am with you always, to the end of age."*

Allow weakness to be a thing of the past and do not allow people to enter into your life or your household and capture you because of your weakness. Women who are weak are constantly weighted down with loneliness, lust, lack of money and etc. Don't be led by emotions or impulses that will cause sin in your life, and don't become a prisoner or become foolish in evil decisions. Ask God to come in your life and allow the *"Holy Spirit"* to live in you and have dominion over your life. Let your day begin and end with thanksgiving to God for making your wiser and stronger as you make decisions in your daily life. Be strong in the Lord, be encouraged and aspire to do what is pleasing to God. Do not allow your decisions or your actions cause others label you as a **"silly woman"**!

THE END

"You Must Wait – Lady In Waiting"

Wait! I say on the Lord.
Be encouraged and He shall strengthen your heart.
Wait! I say on the Lord.

You must wait on God
He will complete a task from within you.
You must wait on God
To unravel the threads of hurt, disappointment life brought
You must wait on God
To prune the branches so you can bear good fruit.
You must wait on God
To learn of His word, strength and power
You must wait on God
To reveal your true purpose-your ministry
You must wait on God
For the one He has selected to your husband
You must wait on God
Becoming intimate with Him first
You must wait on God
For if you can't obey the Word how can you your mate
You must wait on God
Giving Him the best of our services
You must wait on God
As He has waited on you to accept His Son-Jesus
You must wait on God
And I am Lady in waiting!

Wait! I say on the Lord.
Be encouraged and He shall strengthen your heart.
Wait! I say on the Lord.

C. J. Simmons
(Cynthia Jaurdon-Simmons)

Divinely Inspired © 1999

The Author

Rita Jones Rushing is a born again Christian woman who has been born again since 1998. After totally surrendering her life to Jesus Christ, she accepted God's call on her life and to walk in obedience. After more than five years of God waking her up in the middle of the night to write, the Lord said "you must write your first book and it must be called *"Silly Women."* She is an active member of St. Mark United Methodist Church. Rita is a divorced woman who has been divorced for over sixteen years, and she has been celibate for over ten years. She is the god mother of Kaylo Henry and Trae Murray. She has an Associate degree in Computer Operations, a B.A. in Sociology and a M.A. in History from Southern University A& M College in Baton Rouge. She is a full time history instructor at Baton Rouge Community College located in Baton Rouge, Louisiana and she currently resides in Baton Rouge, Louisiana.

LaVergne, TN USA
26 October 2009
161995LV00002B/113/P